INTRODUCTION
TO
BASIC

HARCOURT BRACE JOVANOVICH COLLEGE OUTLINE SERIES

INTRODUCTION TO BASIC

Charles B. Kreitzberg

Cognetics Corporation

Norman T. Carpenter

Franklin Computer Corporation

Books for Professionals
Harcourt Brace Jovanovich, Publishers
San Diego   New York   London

Permissions Department
Harcourt Brace Jovanovich, Publishers
8th Floor
Orlando, Florida 32887

Printed in the United States of America

Library of Congress Cataloging in Publication Data

Kreitzberg, Charles B.
  Introduction to BASIC

  (College outline series)   (Books for professionals)
  Includes index.
  1. Basic (Computer program language) I. Title.
II. Series. III. Series: Books for professionals.
QA76.73.B3K74   1984   001.64′24   83-22701

ISBN 0-15-600034-2

First edition

D E F G H

To Jonathan: Welcome to the World — C.B.K.
To my wife, Dolores Cox — N.T.C.

PREFACE

The purpose of this book is to present an introductory course in BASIC programming in the clear, concise format of an outline. Although comprehensive enough to be used by itself for independent study, this outline can also be used as a supplement to college courses and textbooks on the subject. The topics are organized in a manner that will help you locate the specific items and concepts that you need to study and to enable you to bypass those that may not be covered in your text or course.

The text comprises ten chapters. The first two chapters provide an introduction to fundamental computer concepts and the BASIC language. Chapters 3 through 10 give a detailed presentation of the essential aspects of BASIC programming, including statements, expressions and functions, decisions and control, loops, subscripted variables, advanced control structures, integer, real, and double-precision values, files, and graphics and screen control. These chapters offer numerous examples to help illustrate the concepts presented and to explain how you can use these concepts in writing your own BASIC programs.

At the end of each chapter are special features that are designed to enhance and increase your understanding of BASIC programming:

RAISE YOUR GRADES   This feature consists of a checkmarked list of open-ended questions to help you assimilate the material you have just studied. These questions invite you to compare concepts, interpret ideas, and examine the whys and wherefores of chapter material.

SUMMARY   This feature consists of a brief restatement of the main ideas in each chapter, including definitions of key terms. Because it is presented in the efficient form of a numbered list, you can use it to refresh your memory quickly and to check your recall of chapter material.

RAPID REVIEW   Like the summary, this feature is designed to provide you with a quick review of the principles presented in the body of each chapter. Consisting primarily of true-false, multiple-choice, and fill-in-the-blank questions, it allows you to test your retention and reinforce your learning at the same time.

SOLVED PROBLEMS   This feature consists of practical problems and their step-by-step solutions. Undoubtedly the most valuable feature of the outline, these problems allow you to creatively apply your knowledge of BASIC programming theory to numerous concrete situations. To make the most of these problems, try writing your own solutions first. Then compare your answers to the detailed solutions provided in the book.

Of course, there are other features of this outline that you will find helpful, too. One is the outline format itself, which serves both as a clear guide to important ideas and as a convenient structure upon which to organize your knowledge. Another is the attention devoted to scope and methodology. Yet a third are the many sample BASIC statements and programs that are used throughout the book to help explain and illustrate BASIC programming style and techniques.

Even if you have no previous experience in computer programming, this book will help acquaint you with the concepts and techniques you will need to be a proficient BASIC programmer.

CONTENTS

1 FUNDAMENTAL COMPUTER CONCEPTS

THIS CHAPTER IS ABOUT

- ☑ **The Microcomputer Revolution**
- ☑ **Computers and Programs**
- ☑ **Computer Organization and Operation**
- ☑ **Input/Output Devices**
- ☑ **Terminals**

1-1. The Microcomputer Revolution

Although the theoretical concepts underlying the operation of computers go back a century and a half, the first truly electronic computer was built only in the 1940s. Early computers were enormous consumers of space, programming time, electricity, and air conditioning. Since then, computers have become faster, more sophisticated, smaller, cheaper, and easier to use.

A. The development of the electronic chip was a major step in the evolution of the computer.

The *chip* is an electronic microcircuit, complete with resistors, capacitors, and transistors, printed on a tiny wafer of silicon just one-sixteenth of an inch square. The circuits are so minute that they are visible only under a powerful microscope. A *microprocessor* is a computer on a chip. It costs only a few dollars and may be as powerful as one of the early, room-sized computers.

1. To understand the evolution of the microelectronic chip, consider that early integrated computer circuits were as intricate as, say, a map of a small town reduced to the size of your fingernail. Today's circuits are as intricate as a map of New York City on your fingernail, and tomorrow's are likely to be comparable to the map of North America.
2. Reducing the size of the circuit not only makes the computer smaller, but it also increases the speed of calculation (because the electric impulses have a shorter distance to travel), and decreases the power requirements. Cost is reduced because the entire circuit is mass-produced by machinery rather than assembled by hand. As a result, the computing power that once filled a room and cost $500,000 can now fit easily on a desktop and cost $2,000 or less.

B. Computers are classified as *microcomputers*, *minicomputers*, and *mainframes*.

Only a few years ago all computers were extremely large and required raised floors, massive air-conditioning systems, and special electrical circuits. Today, an entire computer can be manufactured on a single silicon chip.

It has become common to categorize computers as microcomputers, minicomputers, and mainframes. The dividing lines between micros, minis, and mainframes are not always obvious, and the distinctions tend to blur as small computers become more and more powerful.

1. *Microcomputers*, or *micros*, are small and have relatively less computational power than their larger counterparts. The smallest and simplest microcomputers are the specialized circuits that are dedicated to particular tasks. Examples of these *dedicated micros* include computer chips that control appliances, electronic instruments, and various automotive components. *Personal computers* fall into the microcomputer category, but have more power and flexibility than simple dedicated micros. Personal computers are typically used by one

individual at a time. In general, personal computers range in price from $50 to $5,000, depending on their speed, capacity, and associated equipment.

2. *Minicomputers*, or *minis*, are faster, have more memory, and are more powerful than micros. They can transfer data between storage devices and their memory more rapidly than micros. Minis range in price from $20,000 to perhaps $150,000. The lower-priced minis are quite similar to personal computers but offer features that make them more appropriate for business and administrative use. These features include more disk storage, higher quality (and faster) printers, better display (CRT) terminals, and more memory. Higher-priced systems use "hard" disks (which are faster and store more data than the "floppy" disks of smaller systems), printers capable of producing an entire line at once (rather than one character at a time), and sufficient memory to support "time-sharing" (servicing multiple users simultaneously).

3. *Mainframes*, or *maxicomputers*, are the largest computers. Mainframe computers range in price from $150,000 to several million dollars. These large computers provide massive storage and extremely rapid computation. As time-sharing computers, they can support hundreds or thousands of users simultaneously.

1-2. Computers and Programs

A. A *computer* is a device that receives input, processes it, and changes it into output.

A computer does not create information; rather, it transforms input into output under control of a set of instructions called a program. Within the computer both programs and data are stored in *binary* form—electrical voltages that represent sequences of zeros and ones. Externally, input data are commonly found in printed form or as magnetized spots on a magnetic tape or disk.

Input devices transform data into the appropriate form for computer processing. *Output devices* transform data from the internal form used by the computer into forms that can be read by people or stored on recording media. There is a wide variety of input and output devices that can be connected to computers.

1. Input can come from many sources, such as punched cards, display terminal keyboards, specialized terminals like automatic bank teller machines and cash registers, and even from satellite relays. It can come from environmental sensors like thermometers, from sensors built into carburetors and other machinery, from other computers, and from a rapidly increasing variety of public and private databases stored on computer disks.

2. Output can be directed to many devices, such as printers and terminal display screens. It can also be stored on disk and tape for use as input to other programs, or can be converted to electrical signals and used to control machinery and production processes.

3. Within the computer, data are stored in memory and processed in the form of tiny electric pulses that move through printed circuits. All data look the same to the computer, whether coming from an automatic teller or a carburetor, and all data are processed according to the same principles. Figure 1-1 shows how the components of a computer interact to process data.

B. A *program* is a set of instructions that specifies the steps the computer is to perform.

The individual operations that a computer performs are not especially complicated; some examples are adding, subtracting, moving a number from one place to another, and comparing two numbers to see if they are equal. But the combination of many simple operations can produce a complex result. A computer program carries out complex procedures by executing a long series of simple operations and decisions; the programmer's job is to develop the appropriate sequence of operations for the task.

Designed into every computer is a set of instructions, represented as sequences of zeros and ones. Simple computers typically have fewer instructions than sophisticated computers, but all computer instructions fall into one of five classes:

1. *Input instructions* cause data to be transferred from an input device to the computer's memory.

2. *Output instructions* cause data to be transferred from the computer's memory to an output device.

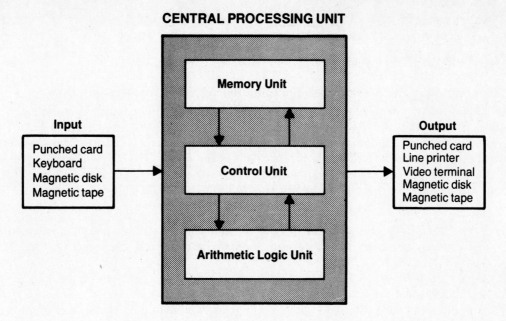

Figure 1-1

3. *Computational instructions* manipulate or transform data. This may be done directly in memory or by moving data into special memory locations, called *registers*, and later returning the data to memory.
4. *GOTO instructions* alter the normal sequence of program execution. Normally, the computer executes program statements sequentially, one after another. GOTO instructions interrupt this sequence and direct the computer to a statement or statements in another part of the program.
5. *Comparison*, or *IF*, *instructions* direct the computer to compare two data elements to determine if they are equal. These instructions enable the computer to conditionally execute parts of the program depending upon the values of the input data.

C. **Programs are stored in the computer's** *memory*.

A program is stored in the same memory, and in the same form, as the data on which it operates. The computer uses data stored in one part of its memory to define the steps for processing the data in another part of its memory.

1. Early automatic processing/calculating devices were programmed by setting switches. As a result, no matter how fast the devices could read input, do calculations, and produce output, they had to stop completely whenever the program was changed.
2. Later computers were designed so that the program could be written independently of the computer ("off-line") and encoded as data in order to be read by the computer at high speeds.
3. Programs were soon developed that would terminate a program when its work was completed and then ready the computer for the next program. These programs, known as *operating systems*, or *executives*, have become very sophisticated and, in large computers, permit most programs to be run without human intervention. Programmers who specialize in writing and maintaining operating systems are called *systems programmers*.

1-3. Computer Organization and Operation

Conceptually, a computer is a device that reads input and transforms it into output under the control of a stored program.

A. **The** *central processing unit* **(CPU) is the computer's control center.**

The central processing unit decodes and executes the program's instructions. The CPU consists of three units:

1. The *arithmetic logic unit* (ALU) carries out the instructions.

2. The *control unit* routes the instructions and the data on which they act.
3. The *memory unit* consists of registers that hold data during processing.

Each model CPU has a particular set of instructions designed into it.

B. The programs and data on which the computer operates are stored in *memory*.

In addition to the memory registers in the CPU itself, the CPU has access to the memory in which the program and the data are stored. The memory circuits are designed so that each individual memory location is assigned a unique number, called an *address*. The smallest unit ("location") of memory that can be addressed is called a *byte*. Each byte is made up of eight bits (binary digits—0 or 1) and can store one character of data or a number from 0 through 255. A computer may have from several hundred to several million bytes of memory.

Memory is divided into two general classes:

1. *Random access memory* (RAM) preserves data only as long as power is supplied. The program can temporarily both store (or "write") data in RAM and access (or "read") data from RAM, as needed.
2. *Read only memory* (ROM) retains its data indefinitely without power, but the program cannot store data in it. Writing data into ROM takes special equipment; hence ROM is typically sold to the consumer with the programs and data built in. ROM is often used to store the BASIC interpreter and operating system in microcomputers. Consumer-oriented software, such as video game cartridges, is produced on ROM chips encased in plastic.

C. Input and output devices transfer data to and from memory under control of the CPU.

Input devices transfer data from an input medium, such as a terminal, to memory; output devices transfer data from memory to an external medium, such as a printer.

1-4. Input/Output Devices

A computer uses input devices and output devices to communicate with the outside world. Input devices supply information to the computer. Output devices receive information from the computer. The term input/output is often abbreviated "I/O."

A. In the past, *punched cards* were the most common input medium.

Punched cards used to be the most commonly used medium for entering programs and small amounts of data into a computer. These cards provide efficient use of computer time because the computer is not tied up while the programs and data are being keyed in. But punched cards are inconvenient because the programmer must submit a program for processing and then wait for the results. Also, the programmer cannot interact with the program to test and correct it line by line.

B. Today, *keyboards* are the most common input medium.

Keyboards are used extensively for program and data entry. In many personal computers the keyboard is part of an integrated system, often all in one cabinet. Although most personal computers support only a single keyboard terminal, many large computers are multi-user systems that support many terminals, all working at the same time—a process known as *time-sharing*. In time-sharing, the computer services one user for a fraction of a second and then moves on to the next user. Because the computer processes data so rapidly, it appears to each user as if he or she has sole control of the entire system. Large computers can support hundreds or thousands of users simultaneously. Even small business computers can often support several users.

C. The *display tube* (CRT) is a common output device.

CRT (cathode ray tube) display tubes, such as the TV screens used extensively on personal computers, and the high resolution tubes used on more expensive systems, are fast, silent, and can often display both text and graphics. The less expensive personal computers are usually designed to be used with home television sets. Monitors, which incorporate screens and circuits designed especially for output applications, provide a much better display than TV screens and are only slightly more expensive. Much more expensive are the very high resolution monitors used with larger computers for detailed graphic display.

D. *Floppy disks* **can be used for both input and output and permit random access to data.**

Floppy disks are 3-inch, 5-inch, and 8-inch disks that are made of slightly flexible plastic and coated with an oxide that gives them a magnetic surface. The diskette is permanently sealed in a square envelope that has an access hole for the read/write head of the disk drive. The inside of the envelope is coated with substances that absorb dust and help keep the disk clean. Inserted into the disk drive, the disk rotates at about 300 rpm inside the envelope, while a movable magnetic head records and plays back data in much the same way that a cassette recorder records and plays a cassette tape. A *directory*, or *catalog*, is recorded on the floppy and is used to locate the files stored on the disk. Disks provide random access to data, because it is not necessary to read the entire disk to locate a desired element. (Random access files and other kinds of files are discussed in Chapter 9.)

E. Hard disks are used to store large amounts of data.

Hard disks, as the name implies, are rigid. Their diameter may range in size from 3 inches to 30 inches or larger, and several disks may be stacked, one upon the other, to increase storage capacity. Some hard disks are mounted in cartridges that can be removed from the disk drive, while others are permanently mounted. Hard disks rotate much faster than floppies, making data access and retrieval much faster, and they can store much more data. But since hard disks are more expensive than floppies, they are more commonly used in business rather than for personal computing. Prices of hard disks are decreasing, however, and they are becoming more common on personal computers.

F. Magnetic tape is a popular storage medium.

Tape was the first good and compact mass storage medium for computers. Cheap and rugged, magnetic tape can store vast amounts of data. Large systems use half-inch tape on open reels, while small computers use various cassette formats, including ordinary audio cassettes.

The magnetic tape used for large computers has proved a reliable and inexpensive data storage medium. Unlike disks, however, magnetic tape cannot be accessed randomly; to locate a desired piece of data, the computer must read all the data preceding it.

Many personal computers use ordinary audio cassettes for data storage. The data are recorded as tones on the tape. Generally, cassettes are somewhat slow and unreliable. Since the cost of floppy disks is decreasing, audio cassettes are becoming less popular except on the least-expensive personal computers.

G. Dot matrix printers provide fast, low-cost output.

Dot matrix printers use a print head with a vertical column of tiny wires. As the print head moves across the paper, solenoids "fire" the wires against a ribbon to print dots on the paper in the form of characters. On the more expensive printers, the print head operates at 100 to 200 characters per second, and prints in both directions. Some dot matrix printers offer the option of printing higher-quality characters, though at slower speeds. This is done by printing each character twice, so that it will appear more solid.

H. Letter-quality printers provide high-quality output.

Letter-quality printers usually use a "daisy wheel" printing element. The daisy wheel spins rapidly as it moves across the paper, and a tiny hammer hits the right character against the ribbon and paper as the wheel spins by. The quality of the printed text is comparable to the best electric typewriters, and the wheels can be switched to provide different type styles. However, printing speeds are typically slower than dot matrix printers.

I. Line printers provide high-speed output.

Line printers produce an entire line of print at once and can print 10 to 100 lines per second. These printers use a series of hammers to strike letters against the paper as the letters move by on a print chain. Line printers are expensive and thus are used primarily on large computers.

1-5. Terminals

Essentially, a *terminal* is any device that performs input and/or output at a distance from the computer.

A. Terminals can be connected to a computer over telephone lines.

A terminal can be connected to a computer over ordinary telephone circuits by use of a *modem* (modulator-demodulator). A modem converts characters produced on the computer into audible tones for output and converts incoming tones to characters for input. One modem is used at each end of the telephone connection. Typical transmission speeds are 20–120 characters per second. In addition to dial-up telephone links, other commonly used communication systems include dedicated telephone lines, microwave satellite links, and "hard wiring" terminals connected directly to the computer by wires. These networks can support much higher transmission speeds. Although telephone and other long-distance connections are expensive, with proper equipment it is possible to access a computer from anywhere in the world.

B. Hard-copy terminals use a printer.

In the past, most terminals consisted of a keyboard and printer. In fact, many terminals were modified teletype machines and electric typewriters. Today, portable hard-copy terminals employing a small dot-matrix printer are common.

C. Display terminals use a *cathode ray tube* (CRT) to display information.

Display terminals are popular because screen display is faster and more flexible than printed output. It is common to find several individual display terminals in an office, all connected to a single printer that provides hard copy when necessary.

D. Time-sharing allows a number of users to access a single computer at the same time.

In a time-sharing system, each user has a terminal that is connected to a central computer, and each terminal is served in turn. The computer loads the programs required, receives input or transmits output, and goes on to the next terminal, all in a fraction of a second.

E. *Batch processing* is efficient for programs that require a lot of computer time.

In batch processing, many jobs are prepared in advance and the computer operator enters them into the computer one after another. Though batch processing is efficient for long programs, it is inconvenient for programmers who are developing and testing programs. Some systems allow combinations of time-sharing and batch methods. In fact, large mainframe computers are usually operated 24 hours a day, so long batch jobs are run at night when there are few users on the terminals.

RAISE YOUR GRADES

Can you explain . . . ?

☑ how the development of the microelectronic chip has affected the computer industry
☑ the differences between microcomputers, minicomputers, and mainframes
☑ the purpose of a computer program
☑ why the stored program is so useful
☑ the differences between floppy disks and hard disks
☑ the differences between dot matrix printers, daisy wheel printers, and line printers
☑ the purpose of a modem
☑ what time-sharing is and how it differs from batch processing
☑ the difference between random access memory and read only memory
☑ the five types of instructions that make up a computer's instruction set
☑ the purpose of the central processing unit

SUMMARY

1. The first truly electronic computers were built in the 1940s. Since then, computers have become smaller, faster, cheaper and easier to use. Computer circuits have been reduced to microscopic size, so that considerable computing capacity can be built into machines that will fit on a desktop.

2. In general, a computer is a device that receives input, processes it according to stored directions, and transforms it into output. Input comes from a variety of devices such as keyboards, punched cards, and specialized sensing devices. Input may also come from the output of other computer programs stored on magnetic tape or disk. Output may be displayed on a screen, printed on paper, or stored on tape or disk for use by other programs.

3. The actual processing of data is accomplished by the movement of tiny electric pulses through logic circuits in the computer. These circuits treat all data the same way, regardless of its origin or destination.

4. A program is a set of directions for processing data. The individual operations in a program are usually quite simple. The program is input and stored in the computer just like any data. Once in the computer's memory, the program is interpreted as instructions to process other data.

5. The central processing unit (CPU) decodes and executes a program's instructions. The CPU controls two different kinds of memory: read only memory (ROM) for permanent storage, and random access memory (RAM) for temporary storage. The contents of ROM cannot be changed by the computer. RAM is used to store values and programs as they are needed, and it can be changed at any time.

6. Input devices are the means by which the computer obtains data and programs. Common input devices include keyboards, card readers, and magnetic storage devices such as floppy disks, hard disks, and magnetic tape.

7. Output devices are the means by which programs store data and communicate results to the user. The cathode ray tube (CRT) screen and the printer are common output devices.

8. Common storage media that can be used for both input and output include disks (of various types) and tape.

9. Input/output devices can be linked to computers through telephone circuits or other communications lines. The modem (modulator/demodulator) is a device that converts characters produced on the computer into audible tones for output and converts incoming tones into characters for input.

10. Magnetic media are used for both input and output. The floppy disk is made of plastic with a magnetic surface on which data are recorded and read by a movable magnetic head as the disk spins. Hard disks are rigid and can store more data and access it faster than floppies. Magnetic tape for computers ranges from the half-inch open-reel tape used on large machines to audio cassettes used on personal computers.

11. Dot matrix printers form characters from dots made by tiny wires struck against the paper as the print head moves along the line. Daisy wheel printers use a spinning wheel of letters that moves across a line, striking the right character against the paper as the wheel spins by. Line printers produce an entire line of print at once by using a series of hammers to strike letters against the paper as the letters move by on a print chain.

12. Terminals usually incorporate a keyboard for input and either a CRT or a printer for output. Depending on the size of the computer, from one to several thousand terminals may be used on a single system.

RAPID REVIEW   Answers

True or False?

1. The theoretical concepts underlying the computer were first developed in the 1950s.

   False

2. Input devices transform data into a form that can be read by people.

   False

3. Computer programs called operating systems terminate a program when its work is finished and then ready the computer for the next program.   True

4. Punched cards provide efficient use of computer time.   True

5. Read only memory (ROM) loses its data when power is shut off.   False

6. Dot matrix printers produce faster but lower-quality output than daisy wheel printers.   True

Fill in the blanks

1. _____ systems serve multiple terminals attached to one computer.   Time-sharing

2. Electronic devices called _____ make it possible for a computer to communicate over telephone lines.   modems

3. A _____ printer provides high-quality output.   daisy wheel

4. _____ memory retains data indefinitely without power.   Read only

5. Today, _____ are the most common input medium.   keyboards

Multiple choice

1. The most inexpensive storage medium for the microcomputer is the

   (a) tape reel   (d) hard disk
   (b) floppy disk   (e) typed printout
   (c) cassette   c

2. Input for a computer can come from

   I.   satellite cameras
   II. environmental sensors
   III. disk storage

   (a) I only   (d) I and II
   (b) II only   (e) I, II, and III
   (c) III only   e

3. Which of the following are components of the central processing unit?

   I.   arithmetic logic unit
   II. memory unit
   III. CRT terminal

   (a) I only   (d) I and II
   (b) II only   (e) I, II, and III
   (c) III only   d

4. Which of the following is an output device?

   (a) keyboard   (d) temperature sensor
   (b) punched card   (e) paper tape reader
   (c) CRT   c

2 *THE BASIC LANGUAGE*

THIS CHAPTER IS ABOUT

☑ **High-Level Languages**
☑ **Compilers and Interpreters**
☑ **The Structure of BASIC Programs**
☑ **Using BASIC**
☑ **Constants**
☑ **Variables**
☑ **Assigning Values to Variables—the LET Statement**

2-1. High-Level Languages

A. High-level, or problem-oriented, languages make programming easier.

Every computer responds to a set of built-in commands. These commands are the computer's intrinsic instruction set, often called *machine language*. Machine-language instructions are generally quite simple, instructing the CPU to perform such operations as addition and subtraction, input/output, data comparison, and data transfer. However, it is difficult and tedious to program in machine language, since machine-language instructions are written in binary code, which consists solely of zeros and ones. Rather than writing machine code directly, programmers often use an *assembler*—a computer program that translates more easily remembered symbolic instructions, called *assembly language*, into the appropriate sequences of zeros and ones.

Even with an assembler, however, most programmers avoid writing in machine language. There are three reasons for this:

1. Programming in machine language is time-consuming and tedious. Even a simple program may require hundreds or thousands of instructions, each of which must be coded individually.
2. Programs in machine language are not easily transferred to another model computer because they are usually designed for a specific computer system.
3. Machine language is machine oriented rather than problem oriented. Thus, many programmers find it difficult to plan a program in machine language because they must think in terms of the computer rather than in terms of the problem to be solved. Also, machine language and assemblers are difficult to test ("debug").

To overcome these limitations, computer scientists have designed *high-level languages* that use English words and familiar mathematical symbols. Each statement in a high-level language tells the computer to execute many machine-language instructions, thus reducing programming time. And since high-level languages are problem-oriented rather than machine-oriented, they simplify program design, making it easier to plan and write the program.

B. A variety of high-level languages are in common use.

Over the years, many high-level programming languages have been developed. Most of these languages are based on standard English and were developed for particular applications.

1. COBOL was one of the first high-level languages and is widely used for business programs. COBOL is a wordy language, and programs written in COBOL tend to be quite long.

2. FORTRAN is another early language, widely used for programs involving scientific and mathematical calculations. Statements in FORTRAN resemble algebra.
3. PASCAL is a relatively new language, developed by Professor Nicklaus Wirth of Stanford University. Named after philosopher Blaise Pascal, this language is becoming increasingly popular for use in personal computers.

C. BASIC is a simple high-level language designed for interactive use.

BASIC is an acronym for **B**eginners **A**ll-purpose **S**ymbolic **I**nstruction **C**ode. It was designed in 1964 by Professors John Kemeny and Thomas Kurtz of Dartmouth College.

1. BASIC is a simple language. It was developed for students learning to program for the first time.
2. BASIC is an interactive language. That is, the programmer enters, tests, and modifies the program at a computer terminal instead of punching the program on computer cards to be run later.
3. BASIC is an extremely popular language for personal computers because it is easy to learn and use.

2-2. Compilers and Interpreters

A. Compilers and interpreters translate high-level languages into machine language.

Computers are designed to read and execute instructions in machine language. Therefore, a program written in a high-level language, such as BASIC, must be translated into machine language before the computer can carry out the program's instructions. This translation is performed by special programs called compilers and interpreters.

B. Compilers translate an entire program at one time.

A *compiler* translates an entire high-level program into machine language at one time, and thus is extremely quick and efficient. A compiled program will execute more rapidly than an interpreted program. However, a compiled program must be recompiled whenever you make changes to it. In general, compilers are used with programs that have already been developed and tested and that require few, if any, changes.

C. Interpreters translate a program one statement at a time.

An *interpreter* translates a high-level program into machine language one statement at a time, and thus is slower and less efficient than a compiler. However, interpreters are often more convenient than compilers because they permit the program to be changed more easily. In general, interpreters are used with programs that are being developed and tested.

2-3. The Structure of BASIC Programs

A. A BASIC program consists of a series of statements.

A *statement* is an instruction to the computer to perform an action, such as calculating a value, comparing two values, or printing a result. Most BASIC statements consist of three parts: a line number, followed by a command, followed by the remainder of the statement. Some statements, such as an END statement, consist only of a line number and a command. Here are some examples of BASIC statements:

```
10 LET A=5
   ↖      ↖
   line      command
number
```

```
203 PRINT "THE VALUE OF X IS", X
    ↖      ↖
   line      command
number
```

```
110 END
    ↖     ↖
   line      command
number
```

B. Every BASIC line has a *number.*

Statement line numbers range from 1 to a maximum value that depends on the particular version of BASIC being used. Personal computers typically permit line numbers to range from 1 to 32767, or from 1 to 65535. Larger computers may permit line numbers to range from 1 to 99999.

Line numbers need not be consecutive integers; in fact, it's better to number lines in increments of five or ten. That way you will have room to insert additional lines later.

Many versions of BASIC allow several types of statements to be combined on a single line. However, most of the examples in this book use one type of statement in each line.

EXAMPLE 2-1: This program accepts a value from the keyboard, calculates its square root, and prints both values.

```
10 REM SAMPLE PROGRAM TO COMPUTE AND PRINT A SQUARE ROOT
20 INPUT A
30 LET B=SQR(A)
40 PRINT "THE SQUARE ROOT OF ";A;" IS ";B
100 END
```

The programmer may now enter a new line, numbered 15:

```
15 PRINT "ENTER THE NUMBER TO BE SQUARED."
```

BASIC will automatically insert this line in its proper place in the program:

```
10 REM SAMPLE PROGRAM TO COMPUTE AND PRINT A SQUARE ROOT
15 PRINT "ENTER THE NUMBER TO BE SQUARED."
20 INPUT A
30 LET B=SQR(A)
40 PRINT "THE SQUARE ROOT OF ";A;" IS ";B
100 END
```

C. Every BASIC statement has a *command.*

A command instructs the computer to perform some action. The following table gives some examples of typical BASIC commands.

Command	Meaning	Example
LET	Assign a value to a variable	10 LET A = B + C
PRINT	Display or print text or data	5 PRINT "Hello Joe"
GOTO	Transfer control to a particular line	100 GOTO 200
IF . . . THEN	Determine if a particular condition is true or false and take some action	200 IF X = 0, THEN X = 5
STOP	Stop program execution	500 STOP

2-4. Using BASIC

On many personal computers you simply turn on the power and you are ready to use BASIC. If the computer uses floppy disks, you may need to insert an appropriate diskette before turning on the power. On some computers you may have to type a command such as "BASIC" to activate the BASIC interpreter. Large computers that employ time-sharing usually require a more formal start-up procedure (called "log-on") in which you establish your identity and authorization in order to gain access to the system.

A. System commands

Any computer that uses BASIC programs must have commands that allow the operator to enter, modify, and save statements and programs. These commands are called *system commands*. A system command is an order to the computer that is typed in by the user and is concerned with the operation of the program; it is not a statement or line in the program and does not have a line number. Although the form of system commands will vary depending on the computer and the version of BASIC used, common examples are LOAD, SAVE, LIST, and RUN.

B. Entering BASIC lines

On most systems you can add BASIC lines to a program by simply typing them in at the keyboard. If a new line has the same number as an existing line, the new line will replace the existing one. Thus, no two lines in a program can have the same number. If the program does not have an existing line with the same number, the new line will be inserted automatically into its proper place in the program. If you simply type the number of an existing line and press the RETURN or ENTER key, that line will be deleted.

   The lines that you enter or change affect only the version of the program in memory. The versions in permanent storage remain unchanged, unless you "save" your work to the disk or tape. (See paragraph E below.)

C. Entering a new BASIC program

You enter a new BASIC program the same way you enter a BASIC line—by typing it in at the keyboard. The program lines are entered one at a time. Remember that when you are working on a program, it is only held in memory. To make the program permanent you must save it to a storage medium, such as a disk or tape.

D. Loading an existing BASIC program

On most systems, you load an existing program from permanent storage, such as disk or tape, by typing the command LOAD *xxx*, where *xxx* is the name of the program you want to load. This command retrieves the program from storage and "loads" it into memory. After loading the program, you may run it or modify it.

E. Saving a BASIC statement or program

To save the program on which you are working, type SAVE *xxx* (on most systems), where *xxx* is the name of the program or the name under which you wish to save the program. If you do not save your work on a program, your work will be lost when you turn off the power. It is a good idea to save your work every ten minutes or so, so that it will not be lost in the event of a power failure, power surge, blown fuse, or computer failure. This is a warning you will take seriously the first time you lose several hours of unsaved work.

   Exercise care when saving a program. If you save a program to the disk but use the same name as another program on that disk, you will erase the old program. Most systems either warn you when this is about to happen or provide a way to "lock" programs to prevent accidental erasure.

F. Listing a BASIC line or program

To list a line from a program in memory you type LIST *xxx*, where *xxx* is the line number. To list the entire program you merely type LIST and the program will be listed beginning with its first statement. You can also list part of a program by typing LIST *xxx,yyy* (LIST *xxx-yyy* on some systems), where *xxx* is the number of the statement at which you want the list to begin, and *yyy* is the number of the statement at which you want the list to end. Statements, programs, and program segments may be listed on a display screen or on a printer.

G. Running a BASIC program

If you are using interpreted BASIC, the command RUN will run the program that has been loaded into memory.

2-5. Constants

Programs written in BASIC make extensive use of constants and variables. This section explains the use of constants in BASIC. Section 2-6 explains the use of variables.

A. A *constant* is a value that doesn't change.

BASIC uses two types of constants: numbers and characters. Any number, such as 1, 14, or −2.3, is a constant. Single characters, such as "A," and strings of characters, such as "HELLO," can also be constants. Whether the value is a number or a character, a constant never changes.

B. A constant may be a number.

[handwritten margin notes: "integer (whole)" "decimal point" "exponential"]

Numbers in BASIC can be written in three ways: as integer (whole) numbers, which do not have a decimal point; as real numbers, which have a decimal point; and in exponential (scientific) format.

1. *Integer numbers* are whole numbers, such as 1, 256, −17, and 27816. They do not have a decimal point and may be preceded by a + or − sign. In BASIC, integers are never written with commas.

2. *Real numbers* are numbers that have a decimal point, such as 1.5, 3.234, and −17.324, and may be preceded by a + or − sign. In BASIC, real numbers are never written with commas.

3. *Exponential format* is a way of expressing numbers that are very large or very small. In general, numbers in BASIC may contain up to 7–9 *significant digits* (nonzero digits or zeros enclosed by nonzero digits). Thus, it might seem that the largest number you could write in BASIC would be 999999999. However, the *range* of numbers in BASIC is much greater than the number of significant digits. On many versions of BASIC, numbers typically range in size from -1×10^{38} to $+1 \times 10^{38}$. Numbers whose range exceeds the allowable number of significant digits can be expressed in exponential format.

   As an example, let's convert the number 40581125646 to exponential format. On a system that allows nine significant digits, this number would be expressed in exponential format as follows:

$$4.05811256E+10$$

Notice that the number has been rounded to nine digits, that a decimal point has been placed to the right of the leftmost digit, and that the notation E+10 has been placed at the end of the number. E+10 is a representation of 10^{10}, which means that

$$4.05811256E+10 = 4.05811256 \times 10^{10}$$

$4.05811256 \times 10^{10}$ is called *scientific notation*, which may be more familiar to you than exponential format. Computers use exponential format rather than scientific notation because most display screens and output devices cannot display exponents as superscripts.

C. A constant may be a character.

Character constants, or *strings*, are letters, numbers, spaces, and special characters (such as $ % & ? ( ) < >). Character strings are often used for titles, labels, and printed reports.

1. Character strings are enclosed in quotation marks. The following are examples of character string constants:

   [handwritten margin note: "1.23" is different from 1023]

   ```
   "ABC"          "Hello Joe, Whatdya Know?"
   "R2D2"         "Oh !#$&%##!"
   "C3P0"         "1.23"
   ```

   The last example, "1.23," should not be confused with the number 1.23. The numeric constant 1.23 is a value that may be used in computation. For example, you may add 1 to it and get 2.23. The character constant "1.23" does not have the numeric value 1.23, and you cannot add 1 to it (nor can you add "1" to it).

2. In most versions of BASIC, a character string may contain from 0 to 255 characters. However, the maximum length of a character string depends upon the particular version of BASIC you are using.

3. In most versions of BASIC, a quote is represented in a character string by two consecutive quotation marks. For example,

   ```
   "He said " "Hello Joe" " "
   ```

has the value

   ```
   He said "Hello Joe"
   ```

4. As this example should make clear, the quotation marks that surround a character string constant are not part of its value; they merely indicate that the characters they enclose form a string. Thus, the character string "A" is one character long and has the value A. The quotes are needed because character strings may consist entirely of numbers, and without the surrounding quotes, there would be no way to distinguish between a number such as 1 and the character string "1."

5. When character strings are input as data, they need not be written with the surrounding quotes. This will be discussed in the sections on data input.

6. It is possible (and often useful) to use a character string that has no characters in it. This string (called the *null string*) is written " " and has a length of zero, which means that it does not contain any characters.

2-6. Variables

A. A *variable* holds a value that may change.

The value held in a variable may change as the program proceeds. In BASIC there are two types of variables:

1. *Numeric variables* hold numeric values, such as numbers.
2. *Character string variables* hold character string values, such as letters and words. (Numeric variables and character string variables are discussed in paragraph D.)

One way to understand the function of variables in a computer is to think of the computer's memory as a collection of boxes, as shown below:

Each "box" represents a variable and can store one value at a given time. For example, the following numeric variable contains the value 64.0:

```
64.0
```

This same variable may later be changed to another value, such as − 381.2:

```
−381.2
```

Similarly, a character string variable may contain the value

```
Handsome is
```

which can then be changed to another value, such as

```
as handsome does
```

However, a variable can store only one value at a time.

B. In general, there are two things you can do with a BASIC variable.

1. *You can assign a value to a variable.* When you assign a value to a variable that already has a value, the new value replaces the old one. This is called *destructive read-in.* For example, if you assign the value 74.0 to a variable that already has the value 38.05, the value of the variable becomes 74.0:

Destructive read-in

2. *You can use the value that is held in a variable.* When you use a value that is held in a variable, you do not destroy that value. This is called *nondestructive read-out.* For example, if you access a variable that has the value 127.0, the value of the variable will not be changed or erased:

Nondestructive read-out

C. BASIC variables are named and constructed according to simple rules.

1. The name of a numeric variable is one letter alone, or one letter followed by a one-digit number. For example: A, C, M, P0, Z9, L3.
2. The name of a string variable is one letter and a $, or one letter followed by a one-digit number (same as the numeric variable) and a $. For example: A$, C$, M$, P0$, Z9$, L3$.
3. Many versions of BASIC allow longer variable names. However, in some of these versions, while the name may consist of more than two letters and numbers, only the first two count, so that SUBTLE and SURPRISE are the same variable (a potential source of error if you are not aware of it).

Consult the manual for your particular version of BASIC to determine the specific rules for naming variables on your system.

D. Numeric and string variables

1. *Numeric variables* contain numeric values, which can be used in arithmetic computations or as output. When you refer to a variable in a program but do not assign it a value, most versions of BASIC will set the value of the variable to 0.

EXAMPLE 2-3: Shown below are numeric variables A, B3, C0, and Z, with their assigned numeric values.

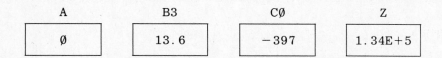

2. *String variables* hold characters. A typical string variable can hold from 0 to 255 characters, depending upon the particular version of BASIC. The number of characters in a string variable is called its *length.* The length of a string variable may change throughout a program if you change the variable's contents.

EXAMPLE 2-4: Here are some string variables and their assigned strings:

A2$

| A□long□string□of□characters |

The length of A2$ is 27. Remember to count the blank spaces between words. (In these examples, a blank space is denoted by □.)

P8$

Handsome□is□as

The length of P8$ is 14

N$

N$ contains the null string; its length is 0. The null string is not a blank or space.

S$

□

S$ contains one space (blank) and has a length of 1.

B$

□ □ □ □ □ □ □ □ □ □ □ □ □ □ □

B$ contains 15 spaces and has a length of 15.

P9$

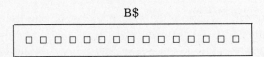

□handsome□does.

P9$ has a length of 15; there is a blank preceding the "h."

U$

5,234,697

U$ has a length of 9. Notice that the value of U$ would not be valid in a numeric variable (because of the commas) but is perfectly valid as a character string.

2-7. Assigning Values to Variables—The LET Statement

The previous section explained how BASIC uses variables. This section explains how BASIC assigns values to variables.

A. The LET statement assigns a value to a variable.

In BASIC, the LET statement is used to assign a value to a variable. For this reason, it is called an *assignment statement*. The LET statement may assign a constant to a variable, the value of one variable to another variable, or the result of a calculation to a variable.

B. The LET statement may assign a constant to a variable.

The LET statement may be used to assign a numeric constant to a numeric variable, or a character string constant to a string variable. The form of this LET statement is

LET *variable* = *constant*

1. The LET statement may be used to assign numeric constants to numeric variables.

EXAMPLE 2-5: The following LET statements show how to assign numeric constants to numeric variables.

```
 5 LET A1=Ø
1Ø LET A=Ø.
15 LET I=1
2Ø LET B=73.7
3Ø LET C=1.7639E-6
```

2. The LET statement may be used to assign character string constants to string variables. The string constant is always enclosed in quotation marks, but the quotes are not part of the value assigned. Using two successive quotation marks within the string constant causes the inside quote to be stored in the variable.

EXAMPLE 2-6: The following LET statements show how to assign string constants to string variables.

```
4Ø LET A$="ALLEMANDE LEFT YOUR PARTNER"
5Ø LET X1$="X1"
6Ø LET M$="""MURDER,"" SHE SAID."
```

C. The LET statement may assign the value of one variable to another variable.

The LET statement may be used to assign the value of one variable to another variable. The form is similar to the assignment of a constant to a variable:

$$\boxed{\text{LET } \textit{variable 1} = \textit{variable 2}}$$

The variable that receives the new value loses its previous value, while the value of the variable to the right of the equal sign is unchanged.

1. The LET statement may be used to assign the value of a numeric variable to another numeric variable.

EXAMPLE 2-7: In the following program fragment, statements 100 and 101 assign the value of one numeric variable to another numeric variable.

```
 8Ø LET I=1
 9Ø LET C=14.3
1ØØ LET A=C
11Ø LET B=I
```

After statement 110 is executed, the values of the variables will be

I	C	A	B
1	14.3	14.3	1

2. The LET statement may be used to assign the value of a string variable to another string variable.

EXAMPLE 2-8: In the following program fragment, statements 120 and 130 assign the value of one string variable to another string variable.

```
10Ø LET X1$="CAT"
11Ø LET X2$="TOAD"
12Ø LET A$=X1$
13Ø LET M$=X2$
```

After statement 130 is executed, the values of the variables will be

X1$	X2$	A$	M$
CAT	TOAD	CAT	TOAD

3. The value of a variable does not change when the variable is on the right side of the equal sign. The value of a variable does change when the variable is on the left side of the equal sign and a new value is assigned to it. Thus, a value stored in a variable remains in that variable while the program is running unless a new value is assigned to it.

EXAMPLE 2-9: The following program shows the various uses of the LET statement that we have discussed thus far. Note that in some of the statements in this program the word LET is omitted. This is perfectly acceptable in many versions of BASIC. The boxes to the right of the program show the value stored in each variable after execution of each line.

Program	Variables			
	I	J	A$	B$
1Ø LET I=1	1	Ø		
2Ø A$="HELLO"	1	Ø	HELLO	
3Ø I=2	2	Ø	HELLO	
4Ø LET J=I	2	2	HELLO	
5Ø LET B$=A$	2	2	HELLO	HELLO
6Ø A$="GOODBYE"	2	2	GOODBYE	HELLO

Line 10 assigns the number 1 to numeric variable I.
Line 20 assigns the string HELLO to string variable A$.
Line 30 assigns the number 2 to numeric variable I, replacing the number 1 previously assigned to I.
Line 40 assigns the value of I, which is 2, to numeric variable J.
Line 50 assigns the value of character string A$, which is HELLO, to string variable B$.
Line 60 assigns the string GOODBYE to string variable A$, replacing the value HELLO previously assigned to A$.

D. The LET statement may assign the result of a calculation to a variable.

The LET statement can be used to compute the value of an expression and then assign the resulting value to a variable. The form is

LET *variable* = *expression*

1. The arithmetic expression appears to the right of the equal sign and may use both variables and constants. BASIC will evaluate the expression, using the current value of variables, and assign the resulting value to the variable on the left. It is also possible to manipulate strings that have string expressions and then assign the result to a string variable.
2. The expression used in a LET statement can be quite elaborate. In this chapter, however, we will discuss only simple expressions; Chapter 3 covers the more elaborate expressions.
3. In BASIC there are five operators that can be used in expressions:

Operator	Meaning
+	addition
−	subtraction
*	multiplication
/	division
↑ or ∧	exponentiation

EXAMPLE 2-10: The following program demonstrates the use of multiplication in a LET statement.

	R	T	D
2Ø LET R=6Ø	6Ø	Ø	Ø
3Ø LET T=15	6Ø	15	Ø
4Ø LET D=R*T	6Ø	15	9ØØ

Line 20 assigns the value 60 to R, and line 30 assigns the value 15 to T. Line 40 multiplies the value of R (60) by the value of T (15) and assigns the result (900) to D. Note that the values of R and T do not change.

EXAMPLE 2-11: The following program demonstrates the use of division in a LET statement.

	A	B
2Ø LET A=75	75	Ø
3Ø LET B=A/2	75	37.5

Line 30 divides the value of A (75) by 2 and assigns the result (37.5) to B. Note that the value of A does not change.

EXAMPLE 2-12: The following program demonstrates the use of addition and subtraction in a LET statement. It also shows how the same variable can be used on both sides of the equal sign.

	I
5Ø LET I=1	1
6Ø LET I=I+1	2
7Ø LET I=I+1	3
8Ø LET I=I-3	Ø

Notice how the variable I is used on both sides of the equal sign. In algebra this would be impossible, since the equal sign denotes equivalence. In BASIC, however, the statement

```
LET I=I+1
```

means "add 1 to the current value of I and store the result in I."

4. Many versions of BASIC use a concatenation operator. A *concatenation operator* is a plus sign (+) that is used to join strings. (*Concatenate* means to link together.)

EXAMPLE 2-13: The following program demonstrates the use of the concatenation operator in a LET statement.

	A$	B$	C$
1∅ LET A$="ABCD"	ABCD		
2∅ LET B$="EFG"	ABCD	EFG	
3∅ LET C$=A$+B$	ABCD	EFG	ABCDEFG

The length of C$ is 7, the sum of the lengths of A$ and B$. The concatenation operator may also be used to combine the values of identical variables:

	A$
1∅ LET A$="BYE"	BYE
2∅ LET A$=A$+A$	BYEBYE

E. Assigning a blank space to a variable

BASIC treats spaces in strings just like any other characters. Consequently, it is possible to assign a space to a string variable.

EXAMPLE 2-14: The following program creates the message NO SMOKING. (□ indicates a blank space.)

	N$	S$	T1$	T2$
1∅ LET N$="NO"	NO			
2∅ LET S$="SMOKING"	NO	SMOKING		
3∅ LET T1$=N$+S$	NO	SMOKING	NOSMOKING	
4∅ LET N$=N$+" "	NO□	SMOKING	NOSMOKING	
5∅ LET T2$=N$+S$	NO□	SMOKING	NOSMOKING	NO□SMOKING

RAISE YOUR GRADES

Can you explain . . . ?

☑ the difference between machine language and high-level languages
☑ the purpose of interpreters and compilers

☑ the difference between variables and constants
☑ how values are written in exponential notation
☑ how values are assigned to variables
☑ the difference between numeric variables and string variables
☑ the five arithmetic operators that are used in BASIC
☑ the purpose of the concatenation operator

SUMMARY

1. High-level languages, such as BASIC, use English words and familiar mathematical symbols and operations.
2. Machine-language instructions are built into the computer and consist of strings of zeros and ones. Machine language is also called binary code.
3. Compilers translate an entire high-level program into machine language all at one time.
4. Interpreters translate a high-level program into machine language one statement at a time.
5. A BASIC program consists of a series of statements that direct the computer to perform certain tasks.
6. Each BASIC statement consists of a line number and a command. Unless otherwise specified, statements are executed in numerical order.
7. BASIC lines may be entered into the program in any order. If a new line number duplicates a previous line number, the new line replaces the old one.
8. System commands allow the user to operate and change the program. Examples of system commands are SAVE, LIST, and RUN.
9. A constant is a value that does not change. In BASIC, both numbers and characters may be constants.
10. A variable holds a value that may change. It is a named location in computer memory in which a numeric or string quantity can be stored and retrieved as needed by the program.
11. Standard numeric variable names in BASIC consist of a single letter or a single letter followed by a one-digit number that may range from 0 to 9. Standard string variable names are constructed the same way, except that a $ is added.
12. The LET statement is used to assign the value of a constant, variable, or expression to a variable.
13. BASIC uses five arithmetic operators: ∧ for exponentiation; * for multiplication; / for division; + for addition; and − for subtraction.
14. A concatenation operator (+) is used to combine strings.

RAPID REVIEW   Answers

True or False?

1. The value of a constant doesn't change.   True
2. In BASIC, the equal sign means that the quantities to its left
   and right are identical.   False
3. The value of a variable does not change when the variable is on
   the right side of the equal sign in an assignment statement.   True
4. T1 is an acceptable variable name.   True
5. LET 47.3 = P*P is an acceptable assignment statement.   False
6. A3$ is a correct name for a numeric variable.   False
7. LET A = "AVERAGE" is an acceptable assignment statement.   False
8. Using the value of a variable destroys that value.   False
9. LET G = "123,975" is an acceptable assignment statement.   False
10. LET 13.5 = 17.6 is a correct LET statement.   False

Fill in the blanks

1. A _____ variable can store letters, numbers, or blank spaces.   string

2. _____ language is built into the computer and consists of binary instructions (made up of zeros and ones) that direct the computer's internal processes.   Machine

3. _____ languages use English words and mathematical expressions, and are translated into binary instructions by compilers and interpreters.   High-level

4. A BASIC program consists of a series of numbered _____.   statements (or lines)

5. Every line in a BASIC program contains a _____, which tells the computer to perform a specific action.   command

6. The _____ statement assigns a value to a variable.   LET

7. The _____ operator is used to combine strings.   concatenation

Multiple choice

1. Which of the following is not a system command?

   (*a*) RUN   (*c*) LET
   (*b*) LOAD   (*d*) SAVE   *c*

2. What would be the value of A\$ following execution of the statement LET A\$ = "HORSE" + "CART"?

   (*a*) HORSECART   (*c*) HORSE CART
   (*b*) CARTHORSE   (*d*) HORSE + CART   *a*

3. What is the length of the character string "Dr. Zhivago"?

   (*a*) 10   (*b*) 11   (*c*) 13   (*d*) 9   *b*

4. Typing the command LOAD PAYROLL, where PAYROLL is the name of a program on a diskette, will

   (*a*) transfer the program PAYROLL to the diskette
   (*b*) automatically duplicate the program PAYROLL
   (*c*) delete the program from the diskette
   (*d*) read the program into the computer's memory   *d*

SOLVED PROBLEMS

PROBLEM 2-1 When writing a BASIC program, why is it a good idea to number lines in increments of 5, 10, 20, or some other interval?

Answer: Numbering lines in intervals, such as 5, 10, or 20, leaves room to add lines to the program at a later time. For this reason, it is also a good idea to use a higher number, such as 10, 50, or 100, for the first line in a program.

PROBLEM 2-2 Explain the usual procedure for loading an existing BASIC program from storage into memory.

Answer: To load an existing BASIC program from a storage medium such as disk or tape, type LOAD *xxx*, where *xxx* is the name of the program you want to load. This command retrieves the program from storage and loads it into memory.

PROBLEM 2-3 Explain the usual procedure for saving a BASIC program to a storage medium.

Answer: To save a BASIC program to a storage medium, type SAVE *xxx*, where *xxx* is the name of the program you are using or the name under which you wish to save the program. Remember that if you save a program but use the same name as another program on the storage medium, you will erase the old program.

PROBLEM 2-4 Explain the usual procedure for listing a BASIC program.

Answer: To list a BASIC program, type LIST. This will list the program beginning with the first line. You can also list a single line by typing LIST *xxx*, where *xxx* is the number of the line you want to list. And it is possible to list part of a program by typing LIST *xxx,yyy*, where *xxx* is the number of the line at which you want the list to begin, and *yyy* is the number of the line at which you want the list to end.

PROBLEM 2-5 In BASIC, numbers can be written in three ways. List each of these ways, and give examples of each.

Answer: BASIC numbers may be written in integer, real, or exponential form. An integer number is a whole number, such as 1, 35, 100, and −734. A real number is a decimal number, such as 1.0, 17.34, −347.932, and 78.3458. An exponent is a number raised to a power. In BASIC, exponents are written in exponential format; for example, 4.58E4, 184E03, 9345E00, and 576E−5.

PROBLEM 2-6 Explain the difference between numeric variables and character string variables.

Answer: Numeric variables hold numeric values, such as numbers. Character string variables hold character string values, such as letters and words.

PROBLEM 2-7 How are BASIC variables named? Give examples.

Answer: The name of a numeric variable consists of one letter or one letter and a number. Examples are A, E, Z3, and M7. The name of a string variable consists of one letter and a dollar sign ($), or one letter, a number, and a dollar sign. Examples are A$, L$, P5$, and R9$. In some versions of BASIC, variable names may be longer than these.

PROBLEM 2-8 How does BASIC assign values to variables?

Answer: BASIC assigns values to variables by using the LET statement. The LET statement may assign a constant to a variable, the value of a variable to a variable, or the result of an expression to a variable.

PROBLEM 2-9 Write a LET statement that assigns the constant 4 to a variable.

Answer: Be sure to use a numeric variable.

```
10 LET M=4
```

PROBLEM 2-10 Write a LET statement that assigns the string "TO BE OR NOT TO BE" to a variable.

Answer: Be sure to use a character string variable.

```
20 LET B$="TO BE OR NOT TO BE"
```

PROBLEM 2-11 Using LET statements, assign 5 to R, 6 to T, and then multiply R by T and assign the result to D.

Answer:

```
10 LET R=5
20 LET T=6
30 LET D=R*T
```

PROBLEM 2-12 Using LET statements, assign the character string "GOOD" to G$, "BYE" to B$, and then combine the two with a concatenation operator and assign the result to R$.

Answer:

```
2Ø  LET  G$="GOOD"
4Ø  LET  B$="BYE"
6Ø  LET  R$=G$+B$
```

3 STATEMENTS, EXPRESSIONS, AND FUNCTIONS

THIS CHAPTER IS ABOUT

- ☑ **The REM Statement**
- ☑ **The END Statement**
- ☑ **The PRINT Statement**
- ☑ **The INPUT Statement**
- ☑ **Expressions and Rules of Priority**
- ☑ **Library Functions**
- ☑ **String Functions**
- ☑ **Defining Your Own Functions—the DEF FN Statement**

3-1. The REM Statement

The REM (for REMark) statement is the simplest BASIC statement. A REM statement does not perform any action or execute any instruction. It is simply a message that gives the programmer information about the program. When the REM command appears after a statement number, the computer ignores the rest of the message in the statement.

It is good practice to insert REM statements throughout a program, to explain the logic and meaning of variables and to describe each section or subroutine. Keep in mind, however, that a REM statement, like any other statement, occupies space in memory. By adding a lot of REM statements to a program you will use a lot more memory. While this is not a problem on most large computers, it can slow down program execution on small computers. In general, though, the benefits of including remarks in a program far outweigh any minor loss in efficiency. (Example 3-1 demonstrates the use of REM statements.)

3-2. The END Statement

The END statement is another simple BASIC statement. The END statement signals the end of a program and terminates program execution.

In general, the END statement should be the last statement in the program, although in some versions of BASIC you may place the END statement wherever you wish to stop execution. Many interpreted versions of BASIC permit omission of the END statement. Since BASIC also includes a STOP statement to stop program execution, our preference is to place an END statement at the end of the program and use a STOP statement anywhere else. (The STOP statement is discussed in Chapter 4.)

EXAMPLE 3-1: The following program is extremely simple. It does nothing at all, since it consists only of REM statements and an END statement. However, the program is perfectly correct and illustrates the structure of a BASIC program and the use of REM and END statements.

```
10 REM This program contains only REM and END statements,
20 REM and therefore does nothing at all.
30 REM It can be saved and run
40 REM on any system, but of course nothing will be printed.
50 END
```

3-3. The PRINT Statement

In BASIC, the PRINT statement is used to produce output. The PRINT statement consists of a statement number and the word PRINT followed by a value or a list of values in the form of constants, variables, or expressions. The statement displays the values that follow the word PRINT. The output may be displayed on a display screen or printed on a printer.

A. The PRINT statement may be used to print constants.

1. If the PRINT statement list contains a numeric constant, the statement will print that constant.

EXAMPLE 3-2: The following PRINT statements print numeric constants. Note that each PRINT statement begins a new line of output.

```
10  PRINT 100
20  PRINT 26.7
30  PRINT -200.37, -341.58
40  END
```

These PRINT statements produce the following output:

```
100
26.7
-200.37        -341.58
```

2. String constants are printed exactly as they appear in the PRINT statement.

EXAMPLE 3-3: The following PRINT statements show how to print string constants.

```
10  PRINT "TITLE    AUTHOR    PUBLISHER"
20  PRINT ""Take my wife. Please!""
30  END
```

These PRINT statements produce the following output:

```
TITLE    AUTHOR    PUBLISHER
"Take my wife. Please!"
```

B. The PRINT statement may be used to print variables.

If the PRINT statement contains variables, the statement will print the current value of each variable in the list.

EXAMPLE 3-4: The following program shows how PRINT statements are used to print variables.

```
10  LET A1=94
20  LET B1=-397.06
30  PRINT A1, B1
40  PRINT B1, A1
50  LET A$="BASICALLY, YOU HAVE AN ACID TONGUE."
60  LET B3$="REDSKINS        COWBOYS"
70  PRINT A$
80  PRINT B3$
90  END
```

This program produces the following output:

```
94          -397.Ø6
-397.Ø6     94
BASICALLY, YOU HAVE AN ACID TONGUE.
REDSKINS         COWBOYS
```

C. The PRINT statement may contain both constants and variables.

We have shown how the PRINT statement may contain either a constant or a variable. However, constants and variables may be combined in a single PRINT statement.

EXAMPLE 3-5: The following program shows how constants and variables may be combined in PRINT statements:

```
1Ø N=7
2Ø N2=N*N
3Ø PRINT "N IS", N
4Ø PRINT "N SQUARED IS", N2
5Ø END
```

This program produces the following output:

```
N IS          7
N SQUARED IS          49
```

D. Rules for printed output

1. Each PRINT statement normally prints a new line.

EXAMPLE 3-6: The program

```
1Ø LET A=1
2Ø LET B=2
3Ø PRINT A
4Ø PRINT B
5Ø END
```

will print

```
1
2
```

2. The commas that separate the items in the list are like the tab key on a typewriter. The PRINT statement prints each item according to its "tab" position.

EXAMPLE 3-7: The program

```
1Ø LET A=1
2Ø LET B=2
3Ø PRINT "A", "B"
4Ø PRINT A, B
5Ø END
```

will print

```
A          B
1          2
```

The spacing between characters may vary, depending upon the particular version of BASIC you are using.

3. If there are too many items to fit on one line, the PRINT statement will generate two (or more) lines.

EXAMPLE 3-8: The program

```
10  LET A=1
20  LET B=2
30  PRINT A,B,A,B,A,B
40  END
```

will print

```
1          2          1
2          1          2
```

with , (commas) lots of space.

4. If semicolons separate the items in the PRINT list, the statement will print the values close together. Numeric quantities (either constants or variables) will be separated by a space or two. Strings will not be separated, but printed end to end.

EXAMPLE 3-9: The program

```
10  LET A=26
20  LET B=32
30  LET C=41
40  LET T$="THREE"
50  PRINT A;B;C
60  PRINT "ONE"; "TWO"; T$
```

will print

```
26  32  41
ONETWOTHREE
```

The semicolon is especially useful when combining numeric and string values because it eliminates extra spaces, as shown in the following program:

```
5 LET A=1
10 PRINT "You are my ", A, " and only."
20 PRINT "You are my "; A; " and only."
30 END
```

Statement 10 uses commas to combine numeric and string variables. Its output will be

```
You are my          1          and only.
```

Statement 20, however, uses semicolons. Its output will be

```
You are my 1 and only.
```

5. Commas and semicolons may be combined in the same PRINT list.
6. As mentioned earlier, each PRINT statement normally prints a new line. However, if a PRINT statement ends with a comma or semicolon, the next PRINT statement is continued on the same line.

EXAMPLE 3-10: The program

```
10 PRINT "This line ends with a semicolon";
20 PRINT ", so all output is on one line."
```

will print

```
This line ends with a semicolon, so all output is on one line.
```

7. A PRINT statement without a list produces a blank line or terminates a previous PRINT statement that ended with a comma or semicolon.

EXAMPLE 3-11: The program

```
10 PRINT "LINE 1"
20 PRINT "LINE 2"
30 PRINT
40 PRINT "LINE 4"
50 PRINT "LINE 5"
60 END
```

will print

```
LINE 1
LINE 2

LINE 4
LINE 5
```

8. You may perform computations in a PRINT statement. Any expression that appears as a list item will be evaluated, and the result will be printed in the appropriate position. (Many programmers, however, do not regard this method as good programming practice.)

EXAMPLE 3-12: The program

```
10 LET I=5
20 LET J=25
40 PRINT I/J, J/I
50 END
```

will print

```
0.2        5
```

3-4. The INPUT Statement

The INPUT statement plays an important role in BASIC programming. Most BASIC programs are interactive; that is, they interact with the user to receive input, process that input, and report the results to the user. The INPUT statement is an integral part of this process.

A. The INPUT statement allows the user to enter input at the keyboard.

The INPUT statement signals the user to enter data and then assigns that data to the appropriate variables. The form of the INPUT statement is

```
INPUT variable list
```

The variables in the list are separated by commas. Here are some examples of INPUT statements:

```
1Ø INPUT A
5Ø INPUT X1, Y2, Z3
9Ø INPUT A$, C3, R2, B$
```

1. When the INPUT statement is executed, BASIC prints a question mark on the screen and waits for the user to enter the data. The question mark is called a *prompt* and is a signal to the user of the program to enter input. The user must enter numbers or strings that are correct values for the variables in the list, separating the entries with commas.

EXAMPLE 3-13: The following program accepts input values for A, B, and C and then prints those values.

```
5  PRINT "PLEASE ENTER THREE VALUES"
1Ø INPUT A, B, C
2Ø PRINT "THE SUM IS "; A+B+C
3Ø END
```

When the INPUT statement is executed, a ? appears on the screen. The user then types in the input—we'll use 10, 20, and 30—as shown below.

```
? 1Ø, 2Ø, 3Ø
```

After the input is keyed in, the user presses the RETURN or ENTER key to tell the computer that input is complete. The program then continues execution; in this case, printing the total of the three values:

```
THE SUM IS 6Ø
```

2. The INPUT statement accepts numbers in integer, decimal, or exponential form. However, BASIC rounds off or truncates a number that has too many significant digits.

EXAMPLE 3-14: The following program accepts input values for A, B, C, and D, and then prints those values.

```
5  PRINT "PLEASE ENTER FOUR VALUES"
1Ø INPUT A, B, C, D
2Ø PRINT A, B, C, D
3Ø END
```

For this program, our input will be

```
.2391,   -36.735284571,   36.7EØ6,   3.2E2
```

Given this input, the program will generate the following output:

```
Ø.2391        -36.73528        3.67EØ7        32ØØ.Ø
```

The value of A remains essentially the same, except that a 0 has been placed before the decimal point. The value of B, however, has been truncated, so that the number contains the right number of significant digits. The value of C has been adjusted so that only one digit appears to the left of the decimal point. Although D is entered in exponential format, it is within the allowable number of significant digits, so BASIC prints it in decimal format.

3. In most versions of BASIC, character string data may be input with or without quotation marks. Quotes may be necessary if the data contain embedded blanks or commas. In the absence of surrounding quotes, BASIC assumes that strings start after the first nonblank character and terminate before the first comma.

EXAMPLE 3-15: The following program accepts input values for variable strings A$, B$, and C$, and then prints those values.

```
10 INPUT A$, B$, C$
20 PRINT A$; B$; C$
30 END
```

Our input will be

```
comma,      COMMA,     " comma, comma"
```

Given this input, the computer will generate the following output:

```
commaCOMMA comma, comma
```

The blanks and comma in the value of C$ are preserved because the input was enclosed in quotes.

4. If the user doesn't enter enough data for all the variables in the list of the INPUT statement, BASIC will respond with an additional prompt (often a double question mark or the word MORE?) until all requested values have been entered. If too many values are entered, the excess values will be ignored, usually with a warning message, such as "TOO MUCH DATA. EXTRA IGNORED."

EXAMPLE 3-16: The following program requests more data if the user does not enter enough values.

```
5  PRINT "PLEASE ENTER THREE VALUES"
10 INPUT A, B, C
20 PRINT A, B, C
30 END
```

If the user enters only two values, such as

```
3.7, 17
```

Some versions of BASIC will print ?? to direct the user to enter the final value:

```
?? 28
```

The program would then print the three values:

```
3.7         17          28
```

EXAMPLE 3-17: This program shows what happens when the user enters too much data.

```
5  PRINT "PLEASE ENTER THREE VALUES"
10 INPUT D, E, F
20 PRINT D, E, F
30 END
```

Given the input

    5, 8, 2, 9

the computer will read the first three values and print the message

    EXTRA IGNORED

The program will then print the first three values:

    5   8   2

5. If the user enters improper characters, such as a letter instead of a comma or vice versa, BASIC will print a warning message and repeat the INPUT statement.

EXAMPLE 3-18: For the following program we will assume that the values of A and B must be numbers.

```
5  PRINT "PLEASE ENTER TWO VALUES"
1Ø INPUT A, B
2Ø PRINT A, B
3Ø PRINT "Thank you"
```

If you enter

    Z, Y

Some versions of BASIC will print the message

    REDO FROM START?

You can then enter the acceptable numeric values, such as

    15, 25

and the program will print

    15   25
    Thank you

B. It is useful to create message prompts.

The single question mark prompt does not tell the user the type or form of the input required. Thus, it is helpful to use prompts that print messages. (In fact, it is poor programming practice not to include a prompt when requesting input from the user.) This is often accomplished by pairing the INPUT statement with one or more PRINT statements.

EXAMPLE 3-19: The following program uses three PRINT statements to produce a message prompt.

```
1Ø REM EXAMPLE OF AN INPUT PROMPT
2Ø PRINT "PLEASE ENTER RATE AND TIME"
3Ø PRINT "SEPARATED BY A COMMA"
4Ø PRINT "THEN PRESS RETURN";
5Ø INPUT R, T
6Ø D=R*T
65 PRINT
7Ø PRINT "DISTANCE TRAVELED WAS" ;D
8Ø END
```

This program will produce the following message prompt:

```
PLEASE ENTER RATE AND TIME
SEPARATED BY A COMMA
THEN PRESS RETURN?
```

The user then types in the input, such as

```
THEN PRESS RETURN? 55, 3
```

and the program genrates the output:

```
DISTANCE TRAVELED WAS 165
```

In this program, PRINT statements 20, 30, and 40 produce the prompt. Note that PRINT statement 40 ends with a semicolon, so that the ? generated by the INPUT statement appears on the same line. The PRINT statement at line 65 generates a blank line.

EXAMPLE 3-20: This program produces a short prompt, which is phrased as a question and thus makes use of the question mark generated by the INPUT statement.

```
100 REM SHORT PROMPT
110 PRINT "WHAT IS YOUR NAME";
120 INPUT N$
130 PRINT
140 PRINT "HELLO_"; N$
150 END
```

This program produces the prompt

```
WHAT IS YOUR NAME?
```

The user then enters the appropriate response

```
WHAT IS YOUR NAME? MARY
```

and the program prints

```
HELLO MARY
```

The semicolon at the end of the PRINT statement in line 110 causes the question mark produced by the INPUT statement to be printed at the end of the message. Without this semicolon at the end of the PRINT statement, BASIC will print the question mark on the next line.

C. It is possible to include a message prompt in the INPUT statement.

In some versions of BASIC, a message prompt may be placed in the INPUT statement, directly after the word INPUT. The message is separated from the variable list by a semicolon.

EXAMPLE 3-21: The following program has a message prompt in the INPUT statement.

```
10 REM PROMPT WITHIN INPUT
20 INPUT "Enter your name and age"; N$, A
30 PRINT "Your name is "; N$; "and your age is "; A; "."
40 END
```

This program generates the prompt

    Enter your name and age?

to which the user responds accordingly:

    Enter your name and age? Vladimir, 24

The program then prints the result:

    Your name is Vladimir and your age is 24.

3-5. Expressions and Rules of Priority

A. An expression in BASIC may contain more than one operation.

The mathematical expressions discussed in Chapter 2 were each limited to a single arithmetic operation. However, BASIC can perform many operations in a single expression. Recall that BASIC uses five arithmetic operations: exponentiation, multiplication, division, addition, and subtraction. These operations may be combined within an expression in any number of ways.

B. Operations are performed in a certain order.

Within an expression, the operations are evaluated and performed in a specific order.

1. If only addition and subtraction are involved, the operations are performed from left to right. For example, the statement

        1Ø LET I=A-B+C

is evaluated as if it were written

        1Ø LET I=(A-B)+C

The following example shows how a longer expression is evaluated.

        1Ø LET B =   2 - 3 + 5 + 2 - 7 + 6 - 5 - 4
                     2 - 3
                         -1 + 5
                             +4 + 2
                                 +6 - 7
                                     -1 + 6
                                         +5 - 5
                                             Ø - 4
                                                 -4

The value of the expression is -4, which is then assigned to the variable B.

EXAMPLE 3-22: The following program illustrates how the values in variables A and I change as they are added and subtracted in statements 40, 50, and 60.

	A	I
2Ø LET A=3	3	Ø
3Ø LET I=1	3	1
4Ø LET I=I+1	3	2
5Ø LET A=6+I-4	4	2
6Ø LET I=I+I+I+I	4	8
7Ø END		

2. If only multiplication and division are involved, the operations are also performed from left to right. For example, the statement

```
1Ø LET Q=A*B/C
```

is evaluated as if it were written

```
1Ø LET Q=(A*B)/C
```

The following example shows how a longer expression is evaluated.

```
1Ø LET B =  2 * 6 / 3 / 4 * 5 / 2
               2 * 6
                  12 / 3
                       4 / 4
                           1 * 5
                               5 / 2
                                  2.5
```

The value assigned to B is 2.5.

EXAMPLE 3-23: The following program illustrates how the values in variables A and I change as they are multiplied and divided in statements 30 through 50.

	A	I
1Ø LET A=5	5	Ø
2Ø LET I=2	5	2
3Ø LET A=A*I/2*8	4Ø	2
4Ø LET I=A/1Ø*3	4Ø	12
5Ø LET I=A/.2/2Ø	4Ø	1Ø

3. Unlike the other operations, exponentiation proceeds from right to left. In BASIC, the symbol ^ or ↑ denotes an exponent. For example, 2^4 in BASIC is the same as 2^4 in algebraic notation. An example of a multiple exponent in BASIC is 3^3^2, which is evaluated from right to left as follows:

$$3^3{}^2 = 3^9 = 19683$$

First, the exponent 3 is raised to the second power, which results in an exponent of 9. Then, 3 is raised to the ninth power, which results in 19,683.

C. There are rules of priority for operators.

Thus far, we have discussed the ways in which BASIC evaluates simple expressions involving a single level of operation: addition and/or subtraction, multiplication and/or division, and exponentiation. However, BASIC expressions may consist of any combination of operators from these three levels. For these expressions, it is essential to know which operations are performed first. For example, the statement

```
A=B*C+D*E
```

could be interpreted in several ways:

$$a = b(c + de)$$
$$a = (bc) + (de)$$
$$a = b(c + d)e$$

This type of ambiguity is resolved by applying the rules of priority. These rules are as follows: All exponentiation is performed first, followed by multiplication and division, and then addition

and subtraction; within each group, as mentioned earlier, the operations are evaluated from left to right in the expression, except for multiple exponentiation, which is evaluated from right to left. The levels of priority are shown below.

> First priority: exponentiation ($^\wedge$ ↑)
> Second priority: multiplication/division (∗ /)
> Third priority: addition/subtraction (+ −)

The rules of priority govern the evaluation of any expression, so that the result will always be the same. Note that the priority of operators has been defined so that arithmetic expressions are evaluated the way you would expect. For example, the algebraic expression

$$x = ab + cd$$

is interpreted

$$x = (ab) + (cd)$$

Similarly, the BASIC statement

    1Ø LET X=A∗B+C∗D

is evaluated

    1Ø LET X=(A∗B)+(C∗D)

D. Parentheses may be used to modify the priority of operators.

You can use parentheses in any expression to modify the priority of the operators. The operations enclosed in parentheses are evaluated first. For example, in the statement

    1Ø LET X=A∗(B+C)∗D

B + C is evaluated first. Had the parentheses not been used, the multiplications would have been performed first, and then the addition. Table 3-1 gives further examples of ways that parentheses can be used to modify the priority of operators in an expression. In this table, A = 2, B = 3, C = 4, and D = 5.

Table 3-1

BASIC statement	Parentheses added for priority	Evaluation
LET X=A∗B+C∗D	LET X=(A∗(B+C))∗D	X=(2∗(3+4))∗5 = (2∗ 7) ∗5 = 14 ∗5 = 7Ø
LET X=A/B+C/D	LET X=(A/(B+C))/D	X=(2/(3∗4))/5 = (2/7) /5 = .286 /5 = .Ø57
LET X=A∗B−C∗D	LET X=(A∗(B−C))∗D	X=(2∗(3−4))∗5 = (2∗ −1) ∗5 = −2 ∗5 = −1Ø
LET X=B$^\wedge$A∗C	LET X=B$^\wedge$(A∗C)	X=3$^\wedge$(2∗4) = 3$^\wedge$ 8 = 6561
LET X=B$^\wedge$A+D$^\wedge$A	LET X=(B$^\wedge$(A+D))$^\wedge$A	X=(3$^\wedge$(2+5))$^\wedge$2 = (3$^\wedge$ 7) $^\wedge$2 = 2187 $^\wedge$2 = 4782969

E. Parentheses may be used simply to clarify the priority of operators.

You can use parentheses in an expression even if they are not needed. This is often done to clarify the priorities rather than change them. The parentheses in statement 20 below are used for clarification; both statements 10 and 20 are equivalent and will execute identically, with or without the parentheses, according to the rules of priority.

```
1Ø  LET  X=A*B+C*D
2Ø  LET  X=(A*B)+(C*D)
```

Table 3-2 gives further examples of ways that parentheses can be used to clarify the priority of operators in an expression. Again, A = 2, B = 3, C = 4, and D = 5.

Table 3-2

BASIC statement	Parentheses added for clarity	Evaluation
LET X=A*B+C*D	LET X=(A*B)+(C*D)	X=(2*3)+(4*5) = 6 + 20 = 26
LET X=A/B+C*D	LET X=(A/B)+(C*D)	X=(2/3)+(4*5) = .67 + 20 = 20.67
LET X=A*B-C*D	LET X=(A*B)-(C*D)	X=(2*3)-(4*5) = 6 - 20 = -14
LET X=B^A*C	LET X=(B^A)*C	X=(3^2)* 4 = 9 +25 = 34

3-6. Library Functions

Mathematicians use a variety of notation to denote the relationship between two variables. You've probably seen expressions like $y = \sqrt{x}$, $y = \ln x$, and $y = \sin x$. In these expressions, $\sqrt{\ }$ (square root), ln (natural logarithm), and sin (sine) are *functions*. The variable x in these examples is called an *argument*, and is the value to which the function is applied.

A. BASIC makes many functional relationships available as *library functions*.

In BASIC, library (or "built-in") functions are used to perform frequently used calculations. For example, a common operation is the calculation of a square root. Instead of writing a long series of instructions each time a square root is needed, in BASIC this can be done by using the library function SQR.

The argument of a BASIC library function is enclosed in parentheses and may be a constant, variable, or expression. The function itself is often used in LET and PRINT statements. Here are the three mathematical functions mentioned above, and their equivalent BASIC library functions:

Mathematical function	BASIC library function
$y = \sqrt{x}$	LET Y=SQR(X)
$y = \ln x$	LET Y=LOG(X)
$y = \sin x$	LET Y=SIN(X)

Table 3-3 summarizes some of the commonly used BASIC functions.

Table 3-3: Library Functions

Function	Purpose
SQR(*arg*)	Calculates the square root of the argument. The argument must be positive.
SIN(*arg*)	Calculates the sine of the argument. The argument must be expressed in radians.
COS(*arg*)	Calculates the cosine of the argument. The argument must be in radians.
TAN(*arg*)	Calculates the tangent of the argument. The argument must be in radians.
ATN(*arg*)	Calculates the arctangent of the argument. The argument must be in radians.
LOG(*arg*)	Calculates the natural logarithm (base *e*) of the argument.
EXP(*arg*)	Raises *e* to the power designated by the argument.
INT(*arg*)	Determines the largest integer not greater than the argument.
ABS(*arg*)	Calculates the absolute value of the argument.
SGN(*arg*)	Determines the sign of the argument. (-1 if the argument is negative; 0 if the argument is 0; $+1$ if the argument is positive.)

1. The function SQR returns the square root of its argument. The argument must not be a negative number. In the following program, SQR returns the square root of a value (V) entered by the user.

```
10 REM USING SQR TO CALCULATE A SQUARE ROOT
20 INPUT "Enter a value ";V
30 LET S=SQR(V)
40 PRINT "The square root of ";V; " is ";S
50 END
```

2. The trigonometric functions SIN, COS, and TAN assume the argument is expressed in radians. A radian is equal to approximately 57.2 degrees. To use degrees as the argument of these functions, divide the number of degrees by 57.2, as shown in the program below.

```
10 LET S1=SIN(270/57.2)
20 LET S2=COS(180/57.2)
30 PRINT TAN(30/57.2), S1, S2
40 END
```

3. The arctangent function ATN returns a value expressed in radians, which can be converted to degrees by multiplying the function by 57.2:

```
10 LET R1=ATN(1)*57.2
20 PRINT R1
30 END
```

4. LOG returns the natural logarithm (base *e*) of its argument. The logarithm to any other base may be calculated from LOG by using the following formula:

$$\log_b x = \log_e(x)/\log_e(b)$$

5. The function EXP calculates the value e^x. The symbol *e* stands for an irrational number whose approximate value is 2.71828 and which is used as the base of natural logarithms.
6. The function INT returns an integer that is less than or equal to its argument. The INT function does not round. Instead, it discards the fractional part of an argument and converts a negative number to the next higher absolute value. For example INT(10.5) equals 10; INT(-2.3) is -3; and INT(-21.7) equals -22.

7. The function ABS returns the absolute value of its argument. The absolute value of a number is positive, regardless of whether the number is positive or negative. For example, the program

```
10  REM DEMONSTRATION OF ABS
20  LET A=14
30  LET B=-14
40  PRINT ABS(A), ABS(B)
50  END
```

will print

```
14      14
```

8. The function SGN returns −1, 0, or 1 depending on the value of the argument. Among other uses, it provides a way of determining whether a quantity is negative or positive.

B. The values returned by functions can be used in many ways.

The values returned by functions can be used in expressions, LET statements, PRINT statements, and even as the arguments of other functions, just as constants, variables, and expressions are used. Here are three examples:

```
10  LET A=INT(B)
30  LET X1=(-B-SQR(B^2-4*A*C))/(2*A)
50  PRINT "SINE: "; SIN(X), "COSINE: "; COS(X)
```

3-7. String Functions

In BASIC, the value of a string variable is a string of characters. The length of the character string may be from zero to 255 characters (more or less, depending on the version of BASIC). Each character in a string may be accessed and put to various uses. This is accomplished by using *string functions*.

Table 3-4 summarizes some common BASIC string functions. In this table, the argument S\$ may be a string variable, constant, or expression. P and N are variables, constants, or expressions. The functions whose names end with a \$ return a string value. The other functions return a numeric value.

Table 3-4: Character String Functions

Function	Purpose
LEN(S\$)	Returns the number of characters in S\$.
LEFT\$(S\$,N)	Returns the leftmost N characters of S\$.
RIGHT\$(S\$,N)	Returns the rightmost N characters of S\$.
MID\$(S\$,P,N)	Returns N characters starting at position P (from left) in S\$.
ASC(S\$)	Returns the ASCII code for the first character of S\$.
CHR\$(N)	Returns the character with ASCII code N.
STR\$(N)	Converts the value of N to a string: A\$=STR\$(N).
VAL(S\$)	Converts a string of digits (possibly with a decimal point, a plus or minus sign, and an exponent) to a numeric value: N=VAL(B\$).

1. Within the limits set by the version of BASIC you are using, the string assigned to a string variable may be of any length, or of no length at all—a null string. LEN returns the length of the string, or zero for a null string. In the following program, the value of L1 will be 17. Remember, the space between the two words is a valid computer character.

```
10  A$="SEVENTEEN LETTERS"
20  L1=LEN(A$)
```

2. LEFT\$, MID\$, and RIGHT\$ pick out substrings from the string in the list of arguments. For example, the program

```
10  B$="ADAMANT"
20  C$=LEFT$(B$,3)
30  D$=MID$(B$,2,3)
40  E$=RIGHT$(B$,3)
50  PRINT C$,D$,E$
60  END
```

produces the output

```
ADA        DAM        ANT
```

3. CHR\$ and ASC are "complementary" functions that allow you to manipulate the character set used by the computer. Each character is represented in memory by a code number. For example, in many computers A through Z are coded as 65 through 90, and the characters 0 through 9 are coded as 48 through 57. These codes apply only for digits used as string characters, not for numerical quantities. CHR\$(65) returns the string "A", and ASC("A") equals 65.

4. STR\$ and VAL convert between numerical values and strings made up of digits. STR\$(41) equals "41", and VAL("32.6") equals 32.6.

3-8. Defining Your Own Functions—the DEF FN Statement

In addition to the standard functions that are built into BASIC, you may also create your own functions. This is accomplished with the DEF FN statement, which allows you to define arithmetic or string operations as functions within a program and then use these functions as you would use any standard function. The functions you define may be extremely complex, and you may define a function in terms of other, previously defined functions.

A. The form of the DEF FN statement

Although the form of the DEF FN statement will vary among the different versions of BASIC, the general form is

$$\boxed{\text{DEF FN}v(a) = expression}$$

where v is a legal numeric or string variable (FNv becomes the name of the function), (a) is one or more arguments and is optional, and *expression* is the function definition, which may be any legal BASIC constant, variable, or expression. As with standard BASIC functions, the functions that you define will be evaluated only when referenced by other statements in the program.

EXAMPLE 3-24: Consider the simple expression $b \times 2 + c$. This expression can be defined as a function in BASIC as follows:

```
20  DEF FNA(B,C)=B*2+C
```

FNA is the name of the function, and (B,C) are its arguments. When the function is referenced, the values of the arguments are defined and then evaluated in the expression. The result of the expression becomes the value of FNA and is returned to the referencing statement.

EXAMPLE 3-25: The following program uses the function defined in Example 3-24.

```
10  REM Define a function with two arguments
20  DEF FNA(B,C)=B*2+C
30  INPUT B, C
40  Z=FNA (B,C)
```

(continued)

(continued)

```
50 PRINT Z
60 INPUT X, Y
70 Z=FNA (X,Y)
80 PRINT Z
```

The function is referenced from two points in the program: line 40 and line 70. Notice that the names of the arguments in line 70 differ from those in line 20. This is perfectly acceptable. The arguments in the referencing statement need not have the same names as the arguments in the referenced function. However, the number and type (numeric or string) of the arguments must be the same. Line 30 accepts input values for B and C. Line 40 references the function FNA, defined in line 20. The values assigned to B and C are then evaluated in terms of the expression in function FNA, and the result is assigned to Z. Statement 50 prints the value of Z. This process is repeated in lines 60, 70, and 80 for variables X and Y.

B. The definition may contain variables that are not defined as arguments.

In the examples we have used thus far, the definition contained only variables whose values were defined by the values assigned to the function arguments. However, the definition may include variables that are not defined by the arguments, as long as these variables are assigned values elsewhere in the program.

EXAMPLE 3-26: The following program calculates the amount in a savings account after a given number of years at a given annual interest rate, compounded monthly.

```
10 DEF FNS (A) =A* ( (1+R/12) ^ (12*N) )
20 INPUT "Enter annual interest rate";R
30 R=R/100
40 INPUT "Enter number of years savings will be held"; N
50 PRINT "After "; N; " years: "; FNS (A1)
60 PRINT
100 END
```

The function is defined in line 10 and is referenced in line 50. Of the variables listed in the function definition, only A is defined by the function argument; the values of R and N are assigned in lines 20 and 40.

C. A defined function may combine built-in functions.

The defined function may be used to create a new function by combining existing built-in functions. For example, the inverse, or arc, sine function is not available in BASIC; however, it can be defined in terms of the arc tangent function (ATN) and the square root function (SQR), both of which are available. This is shown in the following statement, where the function is named FNA9:

```
30 FNA9 (R) =ATN (R/SQR (-R*R+1) )
```

D. A function may be defined using string variables and expressions.

In many versions of BASIC, defined functions may include string variables and expressions.

EXAMPLE 3-27: In the following program, function FNB$ abbreviates string values by returning the first and last letters of a string to the calling statement.

```
20 DEF FNB$ (S$) =LEFT$ (S$,1) +RIGHT$ (S$,1)
30 INPUT S$
40 PRINT FNB$ (S$)
50 IF L$<>"END" THEN 30
60 END
```

Display:

```
Vermont
Vt
MISTER
MR
Hello
Ho
END
ED
```

RAISE YOUR GRADES

Can you explain . . . ?

☑ the purpose of the REM statement
☑ the purpose of the END statement
☑ what types of values may be used in a PRINT statement list
☑ what happens when a PRINT statement ends with a comma or semicolon
☑ how the INPUT statement requests data
☑ how message prompts are written
☑ the rules of priority for operators
☑ the use of parentheses in expressions
☑ how BASIC uses library functions
☑ the purpose of string functions

SUMMARY

1. The REM statement is a message to the programmer that provides information about the program. The statement does not perform any action or execute any instruction.
2. The END statement signals the end of a program and terminates program execution.
3. The PRINT statement produces output. The PRINT statement consists of the word PRINT followed by a list of values, which can be constants, variables, or expressions. If semicolons are used in a PRINT statement list, the statement will print the values close together.
4. The INPUT statement allows the user to enter input at the keyboard. The statement uses a prompt to signal the user to enter data, and then assigns that data to the appropriate variables.
5. A single mathematical expression may perform many operations. Within an expression, the operations are performed in a specific order. Addition, subtraction, multiplication, and division are performed from left to right. Exponentiation is performed from right to left.
6. Operations are evaluated according to rules of priority. These rules are as follows: All exponentiation is performed first, followed by multiplication and division, and then addition and subtraction. Within each group, the operations are evaluated from left to right, except for exponentiation, which is evaluated from right to left.
7. Parentheses may be used in any expression to modify the priority of the operators. Parentheses may also be used to simply clarify the priority of operators.
8. Library functions are used to perform frequently used calculations. The subscript of a library function is called an argument, and may be a constant, variable, or expression.
9. String functions contain and manipulate string variables. These functions allow each character in a string to be accessed and put to various uses.
10. The DEF FN statement allows you to define your own functions.

RAPID REVIEW   Answers

True or False?

1. The INPUT statement allows the user to enter data from the keyboard.   True

2. The list of variables in an INPUT statement must consist only of numeric variables.   False

3. INPUT 20 is a valid statement in BASIC.   False

4. INPUT "Name";N$ is a valid INPUT statement.   True

5. In the statement LET P = P1*S*D1^3/(8*D*K), the exponentiation is performed first.   False

6. In the expression A − B * C, the computer will perform the subtraction before the multiplication.   False

7. If there are no modifications to the sequence, exponentiation is performed before multiplication in BASIC expressions.   True

8. SQR(169) equals 13.   True

9. A − C − B and (A − C) − B are equivalent expressions.   True

10. A^B − C and A^(B − C) are equivalent expressions.   False

Fill in the blanks

1. The value of INT(6.89) is _____.   6

2. Normally, the operations of multiplication and division are performed in order from _____ to _____.   left, right

3. The _____ statement is usually the last statement in a BASIC program.   END

4. The value of 2^2*3/6 + 1 is _____.   3

5. The symbol ^ stands for _____.   exponentiation

6. The value of (3 + 2)^2/5 is _____.   5

Multiple choice

1. The value of the statement 6*2 − 2^2*3 is

   (a) 15   (b) 0   (c) 24   (d) −52   (e) 300   b

2. Which of the following is not a common BASIC library function?

   (a) COS(*arg*)   (d) LET(*arg*)
   (b) INT(*arg*)   (e) ATN(*arg*)
   (c) SGN(*arg*)   d

3. Which of the following is not a common BASIC string function?

   (a) LEN(S$)   (d) CHR$(N)
   (b) ASC(S$)   (e) SGN(S$)
   (c) VAL(S$)   e

4. If X = LEN(A$), what will be the value of X if A$ = "CHANEL NO. 5"?

   (a) 12   (b) 10   (c) 8   (d) 5   (e) 7   a

SOLVED PROBLEMS

PROBLEM 3-1 Explain the purpose of the REM statement and why it is good practice to use REM statements throughout a program.

Answer: The REM statement is a message that gives the programmer information about the program. Placing REM statements throughout a program helps subsequent programmers understand the purpose and logic of the various program segments and subroutines.

PROBLEM 3-2 Explain the purpose of the END statement.

Answer: The END statement signals the end of the program and terminates program execution. The END statement is usually placed at the end of the program.

PROBLEM 3-3 Write a program that asks the user to enter the length of a side of a square and then calculates and prints the area of the square.

Answer:

```
10 INPUT "Enter the length of the side";S1
20 LET S=S1^2
30 PRINT "The area of the square is "; S
40 END
```

PROBLEM 3-4 Write a program that asks for the length and width of a rectangle, calculates its area, and then prints its length, width, and area.

Answer:

```
10 PRINT "Enter the length and width of the rectangle."
20 INPUT L, W
30 LET A=L*W
40 PRINT "The area of a rectangle with length ";L
50 PRINT "and width ";W; is ";A;"."
60 END
```

PROBLEM 3-5 Write a program that asks for the length of the edge of a cube and then calculates and prints the volume of the cube.

Answer:

```
10 INPUT "Enter the length of the cube's edge";C
20 PRINT "The volume of the cube is ";C*C*C
30 END
```

In this program, the volume of the cube is calculated by multiplying the length of the edge three times. Another way would be to raise the length of the edge to the power of three. Note that the calculation occurs in the PRINT statement. While this is permissible, the preferred method is to perform the calculation in the LET statement.

PROBLEM 3-6 Write a program that asks for the radius of a sphere, prints the radius, and then calculates and prints the volume of the sphere.

Answer:

```
10 INPUT "Enter the radius of the sphere";R
20 PRINT "Thank you. I will now calculate the volume"
30 PRINT "of a sphere with radius ";R
40 PRINT
50 PRINT "The volume of the sphere is "; (4/3)*3.14*R^3
60 END
```

Although this program is somewhat longer than the programs in Problems 3-3 through 3-5, its basic structure is the same.

PROBLEM 3-7 Write a program that accepts as input the major and minor axes of an ellipse and then calculates and prints the area of the ellipse.

Answer:

```
10 INPUT A1, A2
20 P1=3.252594
30 PRINT A1*A2*P1
```

PROBLEM 3-8 If you responded appropriately to the following program, what would be the output?

```
100 INPUT "What is your first name?";A$
110 INPUT "What is your last name?";B$
120 PRINT B$;",";A$
130 END
```

Answer: Your last name, a comma, and your first name, with no space between.

PROBLEM 3-9 Write a program that asks the user to enter his or her age in years and then calculates and prints the total number of days, hours, minutes, and seconds in that number of years.

Answer:

```
10 INPUT "What is your age, to the nearest year?";Y
20 LET D=365*Y
30 LET H=365*24*Y
40 LET M=365*24*60*Y
50 LET S=365*24*60*60*Y
60 PRINT Y; " years represents: "
70 PRINT D; " days, ";H;" hours, ";M;" minutes, ";S;" seconds."
80 END
```

PROBLEM 3-10 Write a program that will tell you the ASCII code for any letter that you enter.

Answer:

```
40 PRINT "Enter a letter and I will tell you"
50 PRINT "its ASCII code."
60 INPUT N$
70 PRINT "The ASCII code for the letter ";N$;" is ";ASC(N$)
80 END
```

This program uses the string function ASC to return the ASCII code for any letter that the user enters.

PROBLEM 3-11 What is the output of the following program?

```
1Ø LET N$="CONTINENTAL"
2Ø LET A$=LEFT$(N$,3)
3Ø LET B$=MID$(N$,4,3)
4Ø LET C$=MID$(N$,7,3)
5Ø LET D$=RIGHT$(N$,2)
6Ø PRINT A$, B$, C$, D$
7Ø PRINT N$
8Ø END
```

Answer:

```
CON       TIN       ENT       AL
CONTINENTAL
```

Notice the effect of the character string functions on the output. In line 20, LEFT$(N$,3) places in A$ the leftmost three characters of N$. In line 30, MID$(N$,4,3) places in B$ three characters starting from the fourth character of N$. In line 40, MID$(N$,7,3) places in C$ three characters starting from the seventh character of N$. In line 50, RIGHT$(N$,2) places in D$ the rightmost two characters of N$. The PRINT statement in line 60 then prints the values of A$, B$, C$, and D$, while the PRINT statement in line 70 prints the value of N$.

PROBLEM 3-12 Write a program that asks you to enter your first and last names, and then tells you how many letters are in your full name.

Answer:

```
5Ø INPUT "WHAT IS YOUR FIRST NAME?";A$
6Ø INPUT "WHAT IS YOUR LAST NAME?";B$
7Ø LET C=LEN(A$)+LEN(B$)
8Ø PRINT "THE NUMBER OF LETTERS IN YOUR NAME IS ";C
9Ø END
```

This program uses the character string function LEN to return the number of characters in A$ and B$.

PROBLEM 3-13 What is the output of the following program?

```
1Ø LET A=-5
2Ø LET B=SGN(A)*7+1
3Ø LET C=A*B
4Ø PRINT A, B, C
5Ø END
```

Answer:

```
-5          -6          30
```

In line 20 of the program, the library function SGN returns the sign of the argument (A). Since the value of A is -5, the value of SGN(A) is -1. Therefore, the value assigned to B is $-1 * 7 + 1$, which equals -6. Line 40 prints the values of A, B, and C.

PROBLEM 3-14 Write PRINT statements that would produce the following output.

```
PAYROLL DATA FOR M. SMITH

P        T1        T2

19ØØØ    3ØØØ      1ØØØ
```

Answer:

```
49Ø PRINT "PAYROLL DATA FOR M. SMITH"
5ØØ PRINT
51Ø PRINT "P", "T1", "T2"
52Ø PRINT
53Ø PRINT "19ØØØ", "3ØØØ", "1ØØØ"
```

Statements 490, 510, and 530 print the characters within the quotation marks. Statements 500 and 520 do not have character lists, so they generate only blank lines.

PROBLEM 3-15 What is the output of the following program?

```
1Ø LET A=4
2Ø PRINT "A= ";A,"THE SQUARE OF A IS ";A^2
3Ø PRINT "THE CUBE OF A IS ";A^3
4Ø END
```

Answer:

```
A = 4        THE SQUARE OF A IS 16
THE CUBE OF A IS 64
```

Statement 20 first takes the value assigned to A and places it in the first character string, to print A = 4. Statement 20 then computes the square of A and places that value in the second character string, to print THE SQUARE OF A IS 16. Statement 30 computes the cube of A and places that value in the character string, to print THE CUBE OF A IS 64.

PROBLEM 3-16 What is the output of the following program?

```
11Ø LET A1$="THE MARTIAN I SAW HAD "
12Ø LET A2$="ARMS, "
13Ø LET A3$=" LEGS, AND "
14Ø LET A4$=" EYES!"
15Ø LET A1=3
16Ø LET A2=6
17Ø LET A3=33
18Ø PRINT A1$;A1;A2$;A2;A3$;A3,A4$;A4
```

Answer:

```
THE MARTIAN I SAW HAD 3 ARMS, 6 LEGS, AND        33 EYES!
```

PROBLEM 3-17 Write a program consisting of PRINT statements and an END statement to produce the following output.

```
J O H N  S M I T H
O
H
N

S
M
I
T
H
```

Answer:

```
10 PRINT "J O H N   S M I T H"
20 PRINT "O"
30 PRINT "H"
40 PRINT "N"
50 PRINT
60 PRINT "S"
70 PRINT "M"
80 PRINT "I"
90 PRINT "T"
100 PRINT "H"
110 END
```

PROBLEM 3-18 Write a program that calculates the circumference (C) of a circle given the diameter (D), using the equation C = 3.14*D. Use diameters of 2, 6, 9, and 12. Write the program so that it prints the diameters and circumferences in two columns.

Answer:

```
110 PRINT "DIAM.", "CIRC."
120 LET D=2
130 PRINT D, 3.14*D
140 LET D=6
150 PRINT D, 3.14*D
160 LET D=9
170 PRINT D, 3.14*D
180 LET D=12
190 PRINT D, 3.14*D
200 END
```

Output:

```
DIAM.   CIRC.
2       6.28
6       18.84
9       28.26
12      37.68
```

PROBLEM 3-19 What is the output of the following program?

```
150 REM LET X=362
160 REM LET Y=46203
170 REM PRINT X*Y
180 PRINT "HI"
190 END
```

Answer:

```
HI
```

The computer ignores statements 150, 160, and 170 because they are remarks. Only statement 180 produces output.

PROBLEM 3-20 If you type the following statements and then type the command RUN, what will happen?

```
1 LET X=0
2 PRINT "X IS EQUAL TO ";X
40 LET Q=C^X
```

(continued)

(continued)

```
5000 END
10 LET X=2
30 LET X=C*X
1000 PRINT "X IS EQUAL TO ";X
20 LET C=X
900 LET X=20*X
50 REM Q=9/X
```

Answer: When you type RUN, BASIC will automatically arrange the statements in the correct order and then process them accordingly. This program will produce the following output:

```
X IS EQUAL TO 0
X IS EQUAL TO 80
```

Notice that line 50 is a remark and therefore has no effect on the output.

PROBLEM 3-21 You are the president of Yellow Motors, Inc., and have just found out that some of your cars are defective. You want to notify customers who have already purchased these cars so that they can have these defects repaired. The following program will print a letter that you can send to owners of the defective cars:

```
10 LET S=315264
20 LET D=152
30 LET Q=60
40 LET C$="Mr. Peeblefester"
50 PRINT,,"Yellow Motors, Inc."
60 PRINT,,"266 Citrus Place"
70 PRINT,,"Crossville, TN"
80 PRINT
90 PRINT "Dear ";C$;":"
100 PRINT "    We regret to inform you that the car"
110 PRINT "you bought from Dealer No. ";D;", Serial No. ",S;","
120 PRINT "is defective. Please return within ";Q;" days for"
130 PRINT "prompt and free repair."
140 END
```

What is the output produced by this program?

Answer:

```
                        Yellow Motors, Inc.
                        266 Citrus Place
                        Crossville, TN


Dear Mr. Peeblefester:
    We regret to inform you that the car
you bought from Dealer No. 152, Serial No.        315264,
is defective. Please return it within 60 days for
prompt and free repair.
```

Lines 10 through 40 are LET statements that assign values to the variables used in the letter. Lines 50 through 70 are PRINT statements that print the name and address of the automobile company. Notice the two commas that follow the word PRINT in each of these three PRINT statements. These commas instruct the printer to indent the quoted characters in the PRINT statements. Line 80 causes the printer to skip a line, and line 90 prints a salutation, inserting the value of C$ ("Mr. Peeblefester") where noted. Lines 100 through 130 print the body of the letter, inserting the values of the variables where indicated. Notice the extra spacing between "Serial No." and "315264" in the printed letter. This is caused by the comma that precedes variable S in line 110 of the program. Removing this comma will normalize the spacing.

PROBLEM 3-22 What is the output of the following program?

```
90   LET X=7
105 LET X=X-6
110 LET C=X
115 REM PRINT "C IS EQUAL TO:";
120 PRINT C
130 PRINT "X IS EQUAL TO ",X
140 END
```

Answer:

```
1
X IS EQUAL TO        1
```

Line 115 is a REM statement, so it is not printed. Line 120 prints the value of C, and line 130 prints the value of X, skipping several spaces from "TO" to "1" because of the comma that precedes X in the PRINT statement.

PROBLEM 3-23 Define function FNZ(X,Y) to compute the average of X and Y. Use this function in a program that obtains the values of A and B, computes their average in function FNZ, and then prints the result.

Answer:

```
700 DEF FNZ=(X+Y)/2
710 INPUT "ENTER TWO VALUES   "; A,B
720 LET C=FNZ(A,B)
730 PRINT "THE AVERAGE OF "; A; " AND "; B; " IS "; C
740 END
```

PROBLEM 3-24 Write a program that defines the variable X as $Y^2*Z*3.1416$, asks the user to input the values of Y and Z, and then prints the value of X.

Answer:

```
10 DEF FNX=3.1416*Y^2*Z
20 PRINT "PLEASE ENTER VALUES FOR Y AND Z"
30 INPUT Y, Z
40 PRINT "THE VALUE OF X IS "; FNX
50 END
```

Notice that the function in this program does not have arguments. While this is acceptable in most versions of BASIC, some versions may not permit functions without arguments.

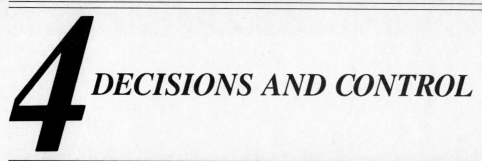

4 DECISIONS AND CONTROL

THIS CHAPTER IS ABOUT

☑ **Program Flow**
☑ **The GOTO Statement**
☑ **The IF Statement**
☑ **Creating Loops with IF and GOTO Statements**
☑ **The IF . . . THEN . . . ELSE Statement**
☑ **The STOP Statement**

4-1. Program Flow

A. Computers control program flow by making decisions.

The power of the computer comes not only from its speed and accuracy, but also from its ability to choose between alternative courses of action. The decision may be based either on values of input data or on values generated in the program. When designing a program, the programmer anticipates the decisions to be made under normal conditions. Good programmers try to anticipate the unexpected as well, so that their programs can cope with invalid input data and other problems, while continuing program execution (or, at least, terminating gracefully). The statements covered in this chapter are the primary ways to control the progress, or *flow*, of a BASIC program.

B. BASIC lines are generally executed in numeric order.

Like English, a BASIC program is read from left to right and from top to bottom, and each line is executed after the previous one. However, program execution can be altered or stopped entirely. It is altered by creating a *branch*; that is, by transferring control to a line other than the next one. In BASIC, there are two statements that are commonly used to create a branch: the GOTO statement and the IF statement. Program execution is stopped by using a STOP statement.

GOTO & IF

4-2. The GOTO Statement

A. The GOTO statement creates an unconditional branch.

The GOTO statement always creates a branch; this is called *unconditional branching*. (As you will see, the IF statement can be used to specify a *conditional branch*; that is, a branch to be executed only under certain conditions.)

B. The form of the GOTO statement

The form of the GOTO statement is

> GOTO *number*

where *number* is the number of the line to be executed next. The destination line may appear anywhere in the program. In other words, GOTO may jump ahead in the program, or it may jump back.

EXAMPLE 4-1: Carefully follow the flow of the following program. The arrows show the branches created by the GOTO statements.

```
   10 REM This is a program with GOTO statements
   20 PRINT "This is statement 20"
  ┌30 GOTO 60
  │►40 PRINT "This is statement 40"
  ├─50 GOTO 100
  │►60 PRINT "This is statement 60"
  └─70 GOTO 40
  └►100 END
```

This program will produce the output

```
   This is statement 20
   This is statement 60
   This is statement 40
```

C. The GOTO statement can be used to create a loop.

A *loop* is a program structure that repeatedly executes a group of lines.

EXAMPLE 4-2: The following program computes the square of a single number.

```
   10 INPUT I
   20 J=I*I
   30 PRINT I; " SQUARED IS ";J
   40 END
```

This program inputs a data value, computes its square, prints the input value and its square, and then stops. The program is capable of computing only a single square, and therefore is not very useful. But by adding a GOTO statement, a loop is created:

```
 ┌►10 INPUT I
 │ 20 J=I*I
 │ 30 PRINT I; " SQUARED IS ";J
 └─40 GOTO 10
   50 END
```

This program accepts input and calculates squares until the user terminates the procedure.

1. Although loops are useful, they can lead to problems if not structured properly.

EXAMPLE 4-3: The following program will calculate powers of the original input until the size of the value calculated exceeds the capacity of the computer system. At this point, the program will "bomb" with an error message.

```
   10 INPUT I
   20 PRINT I
   30 I=I*I
   40 PRINT I
   50 GOTO 30
   60 END
```

Using an input of 2 in this program will produce the following output:

```
2
4
16
256
65536
    .
    .
    .
```

2. A common programming error is the *infinite loop*, which is a loop that never terminates, even with an error message.

EXAMPLE 4-4: In some of the previous examples, the GOTO statement was used to loop back to an INPUT statement. In such structures, if no input is received, program execution will cease and will not resume until input is entered. However, a minor change in this structure creates an infinite loop, which will continue indefinitely:

```
10  INPUT V
20  S=SQRT(V)
30  PRINT V, S
40  GOTO 20
50  END
```

Infinite loop continue printing same values.

In this program, the GOTO statement branches to statement 20 instead of to the INPUT statement, and thus creates an infinite loop. As a result, the program will continue printing the same two values over and over until it is stopped manually.

D. The GOTO statement is considered "powerful."

Programmers use the word "powerful" to describe programs that perform many operations by using only a few simple statements. The GOTO statement is powerful because it can be used to create program loops that execute the same group of statements many times. By combining the GOTO statement with the IF statement, you can create powerful program structures that will execute blocks of statements. (The IF statement is discussed in Section 4-3.) A word of warning: When you use a GOTO statement to modify an existing program, be sure that the GOTO statement is compatible with the program's logic. Otherwise, you may create a tangled mess of program logic.

4-3. The IF Statement

A fundamental function of the computer is its ability to make decisions based on the comparison of values. In general, BASIC compares two values to determine if they are equal or unequal. The result of this comparison determines the next course of action the program will follow. Although these decisions are individually simple, when combined they can result in complex evaluations.

There is no area of programming more likely to result in errors than decision making. In designing a program, the programmer must anticipate all the possible input and all the possible outcomes of the decision-making process. Since a program may make thousands or millions of decisions, and since input data may be erroneous, the results of the computer's decisions are sometimes not those anticipated. There is no way to completely avoid this problem, but careful planning and testing of the program will minimize errors.

A. The IF statement permits conditional execution.

The IF statement is used to execute another statement, called a *conditionally executed statement*, if a specified condition is true. The IF statement asks the question "At this point in the program, is the specified condition true?" If the condition is true, then the conditionally executed statement is executed. If the condition is false, then the conditionally executed statement is not executed and control passes to the next line in the program. You can create a conditional branch by using a GOTO statement as the conditionally executed statement. When the IF condition is true, the GOTO statement transfers control (branches) to another line in the program.

EXAMPLE 4-5: Imagine a "program" for leaving your house on a fall morning. Part of the program might instruct you to put on a coat if the day is cold. This would require that you evaluate the current temperature. Here is a "program" to do that.

> Read temperature.
> If the temperature is less than 50 degrees, put on a coat.
> Open the door.
> Go out.

The program specifies that you are to take an action (put on a coat) only if a specific condition (temperature is less than 50 degrees) is true. The program instructs you to read the temperature just before you leave the house. Then the condition is evaluated as being true or false. If the temperature is 49 degrees or lower, the condition is true. If the temperature is 50 degrees or higher, the condition is false. If the condition is true, you perform the action following the condition (put on a coat), and then go on with the rest of the program: open the door, and go out. If the condition is false, you do not execute the specified action, but merely continue with the program: open the door, and go out. In either case you will be dressed appropriately.

This program can be written in BASIC. In BASIC, < means "less than," so T < 50 means "the value of T is less than 50." The IF statement permits the condition to be tested with the current value of T, which we assume to be the outside temperature. This is shown in the following program.

```
1Ø INPUT "Enter the outside temperature"; T
2Ø IF T<5Ø THEN PRINT "Put on your coat."
3Ø PRINT "Open the door."
4Ø PRINT "Go out."
```

This program first executes the INPUT statement, which prints

```
Enter the outside temperature?
```

If you enter a temperature that is less than 50 degrees, then the condition in the IF statement will be true and the program will print

```
Put on your coat.
Open the door.
Go out.
```

If you enter a temperature that is 50 degrees or higher, then the condition in the IF statement will be false and the program will print

```
Open the door.
Go out.
```

BASIC is precise about this kind of comparison; that is, it evaluates only the condition that is given. If you were making this decision yourself, you might say, "Well, it's 48 degrees now, but the forecast is for warm weather, so I won't bother taking a coat." Actually, you would be adding another condition, which can be included in the program we have just written. Here is one way this can be done:

```
2Ø IF T<45 or (T<5Ø AND F$<>'WARM') THEN PRINT "Put on your coat."
3Ø PRINT "Open the door."
4Ø PRINT "Go out."
```

This complicated condition is fully analyzed in Solved Problem 4-32. For the moment, it is sufficient to note that the program will now instruct you to leave your coat at home if the temperature is

45 degrees or above, as long as the forecast is for warm weather. (Notice that the IF statement can be used to compare words as well as numbers.)

B. The form of the IF statement

The IF statement consists of four elements: the word IF, a *condition*, the word THEN, and a *conditionally executed statement*, which is a statement that is executed if the condition is true. The form is

```
IF condition THEN conditionally executed statement
```

The condition must be a relationship that can be evaluated as true or false at that point in the program. The conditionally executed statement may be an INPUT, READ, PRINT, LET, GOTO, or practically any type of statement (some versions of BASIC do not permit the conditionally executed statement to be an IF or a FOR statement). If the condition is true, the conditionally executed statement will be executed. After an IF statement, control normally passes to the next statement, unless, of course, the conditionally executed statement is a GOTO statement, which would then transfer control to another part of the program. The word GOTO may be omitted, so that the following two statements are equivalent.

```
1Ø IF I=1 THEN GOTO 1ØØ
1Ø IF I=1 THEN 1ØØ
```

Many versions of BASIC permit a third form:

```
1Ø IF I=1 GOTO 1ØØ
```

C. The IF condition is constructed from relational operators and numeric or string expressions.

A *relational operator* describes a relationship between two values. This relationship is evaluated when the IF statement is executed, to see if the condition is true. For example, "Is it *true* that the first quantity is greater than the second?" "Is it *true* that the first quantity is not equal to the second?" BASIC uses six relational operators, shown in the table below.

Operator	Meaning
=	equal to
<>	not equal to
<	less than
>	greater than
>=	greater than or equal to
<=	less than or equal to

Relational operators test any combination of two variables, constants, or expressions. For example:

```
I>J
(I+1)<2
X>=SIN(Y)/2
```

1. The relational operators = (equal to) and <> (not equal to) work very well with integer constants and variables in statements that perform simple comparisons or computations. Here are two examples:

```
2Ø IF I=2 THEN GOTO 37
83Ø IF B<>Ø THEN PRINT "CHECKBOOK NOT BALANCED."
```

However, = and <> should be used with care in statements that perform long calculations with real numbers. The reason is that computations with real numbers may accumulate slight errors from rounding and from conversions from decimal to binary code. Where you might expect a variable to have a value of 2, rounding errors may make the actual value 1.999996 or 2.000002. This difference is insignificant for most practical purposes, but if the value of A were 2.000001, then A = 2.0 would be false, and A<>2.0 would be true.

2. The relational operators < (less than) and > (greater than) are particularly useful where the value of a variable is continually changed by small amounts and when the decision to branch is to be made when the value passes a certain level.

3. The operators >= (greater than or equal to) and <= (less than or equal to) are the inverse of < and >, in the sense that a number that is *not less than* a second number must be *equal to or greater than* the second number, and a number that is *not greater than* another number must be *less than or equal to* it.

D. Relational operators may also be used to compare the values of characters.

Within the computer, characters are stored as numbers. For example, on many computers "A" is stored as 65, "B" as 66, and so on. As a result, relational operators can be used with characters as well as with numerical quantities. The condition "B">"A" is true. "A"<>"A" is false. And if the value of G\$ is "HI", then G\$ = "HI" is true.

E. Logical operators create and test complex conditions.

A relational operator compares two values, such as A = B or T<.05. Often, however, you may need to evaluate a more complicated expression, such as

```
20 IF T<.05 AND I>10000 THEN . . .
```

or

```
20 IF I<10 OR I>20 THEN . . .
```

Logical operators can be used to combine relational expressions to test complex conditions. In BASIC there are three logical operators: AND, OR, and NOT.

1. The logical operator AND is used to combine two relational expressions. The combined expression is true if (and only if) *both* expressions are true. For example:

```
10 REM M is Month, D is Day, R is Rate, T is Overtime
20 IF (M=12) AND (D=25) THEN . . .
     .
     .
     .
100 IF (R>12) AND (T<5) THEN . . .
```

The parentheses are optional, but have been inserted for clarity.

2. The logical operator OR also is used to combine two relational expressions. The combined expression is true if *one or both* expressions are true. Here are two examples:

```
(V<27.0) OR (V<70.0)
 M>150 OR G>12.5
```

In the second example, the parentheses were omitted. This does not affect the interpretation of the statement because logical operators have lower precedence than relational operators, so BASIC evaluates the relational expressions first.

3. The logical operator NOT is used with a single expression. It is true when the expression is false and false when the expression is true. For example,

```
NOT (A=B)
```

is true when A = B is false; that is, when A is not equal to B. The expression used with NOT can be complex, such as

```
NOT (A=B OR C>D/2)
```

but take care that your conditions are correctly formulated.

As with arithmetic expressions, quite complex logical expressions can be constructed with logical operators. The logical operators AND and OR may join logical expressions that, themselves, contain logical operators. For example:

```
I=J AND L<5 OR Q<17.3 AND Z>3.0
```

A few words of warning. The English language tends to use logical expressions in a less formal way than BASIC, and this can lead to coding errors. For example, suppose a school enrolled children who were 5 or 6 years old. In English, you could write

```
if A = 5 or 6 . . .
```

but you can't in BASIC. In BASIC, OR must join two logical expressions. The correct statement is

```
IF A=5 OR A=6 . . .
```

or, with parentheses inserted for clarity,

```
IF (A=5) OR (A=6)
```

Also, in English we sometimes use "and" where "or" is correct. For example, we might say "people need economic support when they are less than 20 years old and more than 75 years old." By this we mean that the group of individuals who need economic support includes those younger than 20 and those older than 75. However, an *individual* who belongs in this group is either younger than 20 *or* older than 75. The correct BASIC statement thus would be

```
IF A<20 OR A>75 . . .
```

F. Relational and logical operators have a specific order of precedence.

BASIC evaluates relational and logical operators in a specific order. The following table shows the priorities of these operators.

Operation	Priority
Function evaluation	1
$\wedge$ or $\uparrow$	2
* and /	3
+ and −	4
< <= = <> > >=	5
NOT	6
AND	7
OR	8

Within an expression, the operations of the same priority are performed in order from left to right, except for exponentiation. When part of an expression is enclosed within parentheses, the enclosed operations are performed first. The number of levels of parentheses that is permitted depends on the version of BASIC you are using, but there will usually be more levels than you need.

4-4. Creating Loops with IF and GOTO Statements

A. IF and GOTO statements can be combined to create powerful loops.

Earlier in this chapter we used GOTO statements to branch back to previously executed statements, creating loops that would run indefinitely. The only way to terminate these loops was by terminating the entire program, either by running out of data, stopping the program manually, or encountering an error. However, by combining an IF statement and a GOTO statement, you can terminate a loop and continue execution in the next part of the program.

B. The IF condition may be used to terminate a loop.

It is a simple matter to terminate a loop by making its execution dependent on the value of an IF condition. Each repetition of the loop tests the condition in the IF statement. Depending on the value of the condition, the loop will either continue or cease. If the loop terminates, control passes to the next statement in the program.

EXAMPLE 4-6: Suppose you are given some money and decide to spend it all. The following program will keep track of your expenditures and notify you when all of the money is gone. You first enter the original amount, and then enter each expenditure.

```
10 REM B is Balance, E is Expenditure, D is Debt
20 PRINT "Enter the original amount:"
30 INPUT B
40 PRINT "Enter expenditure:"
50 INPUT E
60 B=B-E
65 PRINT "Your balance is "; B
70 IF B>0 THEN 40
80 D=ABS(B)
90 PRINT "You have spent all your money and"
100 PRINT "you are $"; D; "in the hole."
110 END
```

The first three lines are executed only once—at the beginning of the run. Lines 40 through 70 are executed repeatedly, because as long as the value of B is greater than zero, the IF statement transfers control back to line 40. But when B reaches zero or becomes negative, control passes to line 80, where the library function ABS removes the minus sign, so that the amount of debt will be printed as a positive quantity.

C. A trailer value may be used to terminate a loop.

A *trailer value* is a specific value that signals the end of the input data. The trailer value is defined in the program and may be any value that terminates input. In this way, the trailer value may be used to terminate a loop and pass execution to the next part of the program.

EXAMPLE 4-7: The following program accepts test grades for a class, adds up those grades, and reports the average grade and the number of students tested. In this program, the trailer value is any negative entry as defined and tested in line 60, the idea being that no student will receive a negative grade.

```
10 REM N is Number of students, G9 is sum of Grades
11 REM G1 is test Grade, A is Average grade
20 N=0
30 G9=0
```

(*continued*)

(*continued*)

```
40 PRINT "Enter test grade (or negative entry to quit):"
50 INPUT G1
60 IF G1<0 THEN 100
70 N=N+1
80 G9=G9+G1
90 GOTO 40
100 A=G9/N
110 PRINT N; "grades have been entered."
120 PRINT "The average grade is "; A
130 END
```

After the REM statements, two variables are initialized to zero: N, which will be used to count the number of students, and G9, which will hold the total of their grades. Line 50 reads each grade, and line 60 tests each grade to determine if it is negative. If the grade is positive, line 70 increments the student counter, N, and line 80 adds the grade to the sum of all grades, G9. The GOTO 40 statement in line 90 then branches back to the PRINT statement, which prompts the user to enter another grade. A negative grade (the trailer value) transfers control out of the loop to statement 100, which computes the average by dividing the number of students into the sum of their grades. Lines 110 and 120 print the results.

Study the order of the operations in lines 60, 70, and 80. These lines are structured to avoid a common logical error. Notice that the negative "grade" that ends the input loop is not added to the total (line 80). That's because it isn't a real grade but a signal to the program. Also notice that the student counter (line 70) is not incremented. The reason is that the negative "grade" doesn't represent an actual student. The grade is tested *before* the student counter and the grade sum are updated. Thus, when the program branches from line 60 to line 100, the accumulator and the counter are correct for the last actual grade that was entered. (Note, however, that the program will "bomb" if the first grade entered is negative, because the system will try to divide G9 by 0.0 in line 100. As an exercise, modify the program so that it will terminate gracefully under this condition.)

D. A counter may be used to terminate a loop.

To perform a series of operations a given number of times, the condition in the IF statement can be set up to test a counter. A *counter* is a variable that is set to a starting value at the beginning of a loop and is then increased by 1 each time the loop is executed. The loop terminates when the counter reaches a pre-set limit.

EXAMPLE 4-8: In the following two programs, I is used as a counter. The first program sums the integers from 1 to 10; the second program allows the user to select the upper limit.

```
10 REM S is Sum, I is Index
20 S=0
30 I=0
40 I=I+1
50 S=S+I
60 IF I<10 THEN 40
70 PRINT "The sum of integers from 1 to 10 is "; S
80 END
```

```
10 REM S is Sum, I is Index, L is upper Limit
20 S=0
30 I=0
40 PRINT "Enter the upper limit of the summing procedure."
50 INPUT L
60 I=I+1
70 S=S+I
```

(*continued*)

(continued)
```
 80 IF I<L THEN 60
 90 PRINT "The sum of integers from 1 to"; L; "is"; S
100 END
```

The second program asks the user to "Enter the upper limit of the summing procedure." If the user enters the number 5, for example, the program will sum the integers from 1 to 5 and then print

```
The sum of integers from 1 to 5 is 15
```

In each program, the accumulator (S) and counter (I) are initialized in lines 20 and 30. In the second program, the variable L is used instead of the constant 10 as the upper limit. The loop branches from line 80 to line 60. Each time through the loop, the value of I increases by 1, and the new value is added to the sum, S. The loop terminates when the value of I reaches the value of L, as tested by the IF statement condition. Notice that the loop continues only as long as I is less than the limit. The last time through the loop, when I is equal to L, the value of I is added to S, and the loop terminates.

E. Setting up a loop with an IF statement, a GOTO statement, and a counter

There are two common ways of setting up a loop with an IF statement, a GOTO statement, and a counter. One way is to increment the counter and then test to see if the loop should be terminated. The other way is to test first and increment second. Carefully study the following two programs. Both will execute ten times.

1. Initialize, increment, test, branch.

```
10 I=0                                  initialize
20 I=I+1                                increment
30 REM Other operations are inserted here
40 PRINT "Repetition "; I
50 IF I<10 THEN 20                      test, branch
60 END
```

2. Initialize, test, increment, branch.

```
10 I=0                                  initialize
20 IF I>=10 THEN 60                     test
30 I=I+1                                increment
40 REM Other operations are inserted here
50 PRINT "Repetition "; I
60 GOTO 20                              branch
70 END
```

The exact form of the IF . . . GOTO loop is up to you. But you should always check the loop to make sure that the counters and accumulators are producing the right answers, and that the loop is terminating after repeating the desired number of times. A common error is to construct loops that repeat one time too many or one time too few. For debugging purposes, it is helpful to include some extra PRINT statements to output the critical values each time the loop repeats. These extra statements can be removed for the final version of the program.

4-5. The IF . . . THEN . . . ELSE Statement

In its simplest form, the BASIC IF statement often requires program structures that are difficult to write and confusing to understand. More recently developed languages, such as PASCAL, Structured COBOL, and FORTRAN 77, offer more powerful structures. A limited version of one of these structures is the IF . . . THEN . . . ELSE statement, which is offered in some versions of BASIC.

A. The IF . . . THEN . . . ELSE statement has two conditionally executed statements.

The IF . . . THEN . . . ELSE statement contains two conditionally executed statements (instead of one) that depend on the IF condition.

EXAMPLE 4-9: The following program uses an IF . . . THEN . . . ELSE statement.

```
1Ø INPUT A
2Ø IF A>=Ø THEN PRINT "It's positive." ELSE PRINT "It's negative."
3Ø PRINT "My decision is final."
4Ø END
```

If a positive number, such as 5.6, is entered, the output of the program will be

```
? 5.6
It's positive.
My decision is final.
```

If a negative number, such as −32, is entered, the output of the program will be

```
? -32
It's negative.
My decision is final.
```

B. Nested IF statements

Some versions of BASIC permit an IF statement to contain another IF statement. The inside IF statement is called a *nested statement*.

EXAMPLE 4-10: The following program has a nested IF statement in the IF . . . THEN . . . ELSE statement in line 20.

```
1Ø INPUT "Please answer YES or NO"; A$
2Ø IF A$="YES" THEN 3ØØ ELSE IF A$="NO" THEN 4ØØ
3Ø PRINT "Your answer wasn't clear."
4Ø GOTO 1Ø
3ØØ PRINT "You answered YES. That's very positive of you."
31Ø PRINT "We'll end on that note."
32Ø STOP
4ØØ PRINT "You answered NO. That's quite decisive."
41Ø PRINT "Thank you for your time."
42Ø END
```

The program first displays

```
Please answer YES or NO?
```

If you do not answer YES or NO, such as

```
Please answer YES or NO? MAYBE
```

the program will print

```
Your answer wasn't clear.
Please answer YES or NO?
```

If your answer is NO, the program will print

```
You answered NO. That's quite decisive.
Thank you for your time.
```

C. You can place several statements in one IF statement.

Some versions of BASIC allow you to place more than one statement on a line. The statements are separated from each other by a special character; in most versions of BASIC, a colon (:) is used. Combining statements in this way can substantially increase the power of the IF statement.

EXAMPLE 4-11: The following program combines IF, PRINT, and GOTO statements in line 30.

```
10 REM Program with multiple statements following IF
20 INPUT "ENTER A POSITIVE NUMBER";A
30 IF A<0 THEN PRINT A; " IS NOT POSITIVE.": GOTO 20
40 PRINT A; " IS POSITIVE, I'M SURE."
```

Line 30 uses a colon to include a GOTO statement at the end of the IF statement.

4-6. The STOP Statement

Wherever it appears in the program, STOP suspends execution. Many implementations of BASIC will display the number of the STOP line when a STOP statement is executed. Thus,

```
45 STOP
```

will display the message

```
BREAK IN LINE 45,
```

or something similar.

STOP is similar to END. In general, programmers prefer to use END as the last statement in the program and STOP in the body of the program. Some versions of BASIC permit restarting a program at the statement following the STOP by using the command CONTINUE or CONT.

RAISE YOUR GRADES

Can you explain . . . ?

☑ the order in which BASIC lines are normally executed
☑ what "program flow" means
☑ how the GOTO statement alters program flow
☑ the form and purpose of the IF statement
☑ the difference between a conditional branch and an unconditional branch
☑ the function of the IF . . . THEN . . . ELSE statement
☑ how to use counters and trailer values
☑ the difference between relational operators and logical operators
☑ the difference between the STOP statement and the END statement

---

SUMMARY

1. BASIC lines are generally executed in numeric order. However, program execution can be altered or stopped entirely. This is accomplished by using GOTO, IF, and STOP statements.
2. The GOTO statement creates an unconditional branch to another part of the program. An unconditional branch is a branch that always alters program flow.
3. The form of the GOTO statement is GOTO *number*, where *number* is the line to be branched to. GOTO 200, for example, transfers control to statement 200.

4. A GOTO statement may branch backward or forward in a program. GOTO statements are often used to repeatedly execute the same sequence of lines. This is called a loop. A loop that does not contain a termination procedure is called an infinite loop.

5. The IF statement permits conditional execution, which occurs only if a specified condition is true.

6. The form of the IF statement is IF *condition* THEN *conditionally executed statement.* The condition can be true or false. If it is true, the conditionally executed statement is executed. If it is false, control passes to the next line.

7. An IF condition is constructed from relational operators and numeric or string expressions.

8. A relational operator describes the relationship between two values. There are six relational operators: =, >, <, <=, >=, <>.

9. Logical operators are used to test more complex conditions. There are three logical operators: NOT, AND, and OR.

10. Relational and logical operators have a specific order of precedence, as shown in the following table. (This precedence may be modified by parentheses.)

Operation	Priority
Function evaluation	1
^ or ↑	2
* and /	3
+ and −	4
< <= = <> > >=	5
NOT	6
AND	7
OR	8

11. IF and GOTO statements can be combined to create loops. The GOTO statement transfers control to the beginning of the loop until the condition in the IF statement is satisfied. Trailer values and counters are often used to terminate a loop.

12. When a GOTO statement is used in an IF statement, the word GOTO may be omitted. For example, IF A = B THEN 100 is equivalent to IF A = B THEN GOTO 100.

13. The IF . . . THEN . . . ELSE statement has two conditionally executed statements. The form is IF *condition* THEN *conditionally executed statement* ELSE *conditionally executed statement.* The statement after THEN is executed if the condition is true, and the statement after ELSE is executed if the condition is not true.

14. If the conditionally executed statement does not transfer control, then control passes to the next statement in the program.

15. IF statements may be nested in the IF . . . THEN . . . ELSE statement.

RAPID REVIEW   Answers

True or False?

1. A good way to modify a program is to insert some GOTO statements to jump to another part of the program. — False

2. Any variable may be used in an IF condition. — True

3. An IF statement cannot be used to determine the validity of input data. — False

4. A STOP statement may appear anywhere in the program. — True

5. The GOTO statement may only jump forward in a program. — False

6. When the condition in an IF statement is true, the conditionally executed statement is executed. — True

7. The condition in an IF line must consist of two variables. — False

8. There are six relational operators in BASIC. — True

9. There are four logical operators in BASIC.   False

10. The logical relation NOT (A<B) is the same as A>=B.   True

11. The logical relation NOT (A=B) is the same as A<>B.   True

12. Parentheses may be used to modify the order in which relational
    and logical operators are executed.   True

Fill in the blanks

1. The word _____ describes a program that processes a lot
   of data with relatively few statements.   powerful

2. Unless transfer-of-control statements are encountered, BASIC
   lines are executed _____ .   sequentially

3. A sequence of lines that is executed repeatedly is called a ____ .   loop

4. The IF statement permits _____ execution.   conditional

5. A _____ operator describes the relationship between two
   values.   relational

6. GOTO 200 causes a branch to line _____ .   200

7. _____ operators test complex conditions.   Logical

8. A _____ is a specific value that signals the end of input
   data.   trailer value

Multiple choice

1. Choose the correct output for the following program:

```
10 I=1
20 J=I^I
30 PRINT J
40 I=I+1
50 IF I<=3 GOTO 20
60 END
```

(a) 1   (b) 2   (c) 2   (d) 1
     4   16   4   2
     27   36   8   3   a

2. Which of the following values would be best to use as a trailer
   record to terminate input of student grades?

   (a) 90   (b) 5   (c) -10   (d) 59   c

3. Which of these loops will print the numbers 1, 2, 3, . . . ?

```
(a) 10 I=1          (b) 10 I=1          (c) 10 I=1
    20 I=I+1            20 I=I+1            20 PRINT I
    30 PRINT I         30 PRINT I          30 I=I+1
    40 GOTO 10         40 GOTO             40 GOTO 20
```
                                                                            c

4. What is the output of this program segment?

```
10 I=0
20 IF I>0 THEN PRINT "AB" ELSE PRINT "BA"
```

   (a) AB   (b) BA   (c) ABAB   (d) BABA   b

SOLVED PROBLEMS

PROBLEM 4-1 What is the output of this program fragment?

```
1Ø GOTO 4Ø
2Ø PRINT "THE FIRST LINE."
3Ø GOTO 7Ø
4Ø PRINT "THE SECOND LINE."
5Ø PRINT "THE THIRD LINE."
6Ø GOTO 2Ø
7Ø . . .
```

Answer:

```
THE SECOND LINE.
THE THIRD LINE.
THE FIRST LINE.
```

PROBLEM 4-2 If any of the following IF conditions is incorrect, locate and correct the error or errors.

(*a*) IF A>>B
(*b*) IF A>B
(*c*) IF K>-I
(*d*) IF (A+)B>C
(*e*) IF P1<=1Ø

Answers:

(*a*) Wrong operator. "Greater than" is >.
(*c*) The operator should be >=.
(*d*) Stray parenthesis. The correct form is (A+B)>C.

PROBLEM 4-3 For each of the following statements or program fragments, identify the errors, if any.

(*a*) 2Ø IF A>B GOTO 2Ø
(*b*) 2Ø IF D>E GOTO 1ØØ
(*c*) 2Ø IF X>Y THEN IF M=1Ø THEN 3Ø
(*d*) 1Ø I=Ø
    2Ø I=I+1
    3Ø IF I<5 THEN 1Ø

Answers:

(*a*) If the evaluation is true, this statement becomes an infinite loop.
(*c*) Correct only in versions of BASIC that allow the nested IF structure.
(*d*) This fragment creates an infinite loop.

PROBLEM 4-4 Evaluate the following IF condition as TRUE or FALSE for the values given in (*a*) and (*b*).

```
IF A>B AND NOT (X>Y)
```

(*a*) A=4.
    B=3.
    X=6.
    Y=5.

(*b*) A=4.
    B=3.
    X=5.
    Y=6.

Answers:

(*a*)   FALSE
(*b*)   TRUE

Here is the progressive evaluation of the condition for the values given in (*b*).

```
IF A>B AND NOT (X>Y)     original condition
4>3 AND NOT (5>6)        evaluate variables
TRUE AND NOT FALSE       evaluate within parentheses
TRUE AND TRUE            simplify expression
     TRUE                final evaluation
```

PROBLEM 4-5 Convert the following complex IF statement into two simple IF statements.

```
1Ø IF I<=1Ø OR T<=Ø THEN 2ØØ
3Ø . . .
```

Answer:

```
1Ø IF I<=1Ø THEN 2ØØ
2Ø IF T<=Ø   THEN 2ØØ
3Ø . . .
```

PROBLEM 4-6 Convert the following complex IF statement into two simple IF statements.

```
1Ø IF A>B AND D<=B THEN 2ØØ
3Ø . . .
```

Answer:

```
1Ø IF A>B THEN 25
2Ø GOTO 3Ø
25 IF D<=B THEN 2ØØ
3Ø . . .
```

or

```
1Ø IF NOT (A>B) THEN 3Ø
2Ø IF D<=B THEN 2ØØ
3Ø . . .
```

PROBLEM 4-7 At what line does execution continue after

```
1Ø IF A>B AND C<=D THEN 4ØØ
5Ø . . .
```

if the variables are initialized as follows:

(*a*)	(*b*)	(*c*)
A=3.Ø	A=6.Ø	A=4.Ø
B=4.Ø	B=5.Ø	B=3.Ø
C=5.Ø	C=4.Ø	C=5.Ø
D=6.Ø	D=3.Ø	D=6.Ø

Answers: (*a*) line 50, (*b*) line 50, (*c*) line 400

PROBLEM 4-8 At what line does execution continue after

```
10 IF A>B THEN 30
20 . . .
```

if the variables are initialized as follows:

(*a*) A=3.   (*b*) A=4.   (*c*) A=123.016
   B=5.   B=4.   B=123.015

Answers: (*a*) line 20, (*b*) line 20, (*c*) line 30

PROBLEM 4-9 Write an IF statement that transfers control to line 500 if I is less than or equal to 3 and R is greater than 3.7.

Answer:

```
IF I<=3 AND R>3.7 THEN 500
```

PROBLEM 4-10 Write an IF statement that prints ECONOMY if speed is greater than 45 and m.p.g. is 30 or more.

Answer:

```
10 REM S is Speed, M is Mpg
20 INPUT S, M
30 IF S>45 AND M>=30 THEN PRINT "ECONOMY"
```

PROBLEM 4-11 Write an IF statement that prints MIDDLE CLASS if wife's salary or husband's salary is $30,000 or greater.

Answer:

```
10 REM W is Wife's salary, H is Husband's Salary
20 INPUT W, H
30 IF W>=30000 OR H>=30000 THEN PRINT "MIDDLE CLASS"
```

PROBLEM 4-12 For incomes up to and including $20,000, the tax rate is 5%; over $20,000, the rate is 7%. Write a program fragment that will calculate the tax.

Answer:

```
10 REM A is Annual income, R is Rate, T is Tax
20 R=.05
30 INPUT A
40 IF A>20000 THEN R=.07
50 T=A*R
```

or

```
10 REM A is Annual income, T is Tax
20 INPUT A
30 T=A*.05
40 IF A>20000 THEN T=A*.07
```

PROBLEM 4-13 What will be the first and last values printed by the following program?

```
10 I=1
20 IF I>10 THEN 60
30 PRINT I
```
(*continued*)

(continued)

```
40 I=I+1
50 GOTO 20
60 END
```

Answer: 1 . . . 10

PROBLEM 4-14 What will be the last value printed by the following program?

```
10 I=0
20 I=I+1
30 PRINT I
40 IF I<=15 THEN 20
50 END
```

Answer: The last value this program will print is 16.

PROBLEM 4-15 What values will the following program print?

```
10 I=0
20 PRINT I
30 I=I+1
40 IF I<=15 THEN 20
50 END
```

Answer: This program will print the values from 0 through 15.

PROBLEM 4-16 What will be the first and last values printed by the following program?

```
10 I=1
20 PRINT I
30 I=I+1
40 IF I<=15 THEN 20
50 END
```

Answer: 1 . . . 14

PROBLEM 4-17 What values will be printed by the following program?

```
10 I=0
20 I=I+1
30 PRINT I
40 IF I>=20 THEN 60
50 GOTO 10
60 END
```

Answer: This program is an infinite loop, because I is reset to 0 and incremented to 1 in every repetition. Thus, the program will print 1s indefinitely.

PROBLEM 4-18 Write a program that accepts input of a real number R and an integer N, and then computes R^N by multiplying R by itself N times.

Answer:

```
10 REM P is Power, N is exponent, R is the input number
11 REM I is a counter
20 P=1
30 I=0
40 INPUT "Enter the number and the exponent"; R, N
```
(continued)

(continued)

```
5Ø IF N=Ø THEN 9Ø
6Ø P=P*R
7Ø I=I+1
8Ø IF I<N THEN 6Ø
9Ø PRINT R; "to the "; I; "power is "; P
1ØØ END
```

PROBLEM 4-19 Write a program that prints the smallest of three input numbers.

Answer:

```
1Ø REM This program finds the smallest of numbers S1, S2, S3
2Ø INPUT S1, S2, S3
3Ø IF S1<S2 AND S1<S3 THEN 7Ø
4Ø IF S2<S1 AND S2<S3 THEN 9Ø
5Ø PRINT S3; "is smallest."
6Ø GOTO 1ØØ
7Ø PRINT S1; "is smallest."
8Ø GOTO 1ØØ
9Ø PRINT S2; "is smallest."
1ØØ END
```

PROBLEM 4-20 When data are entered into a terminal during execution of the program, a well-written program will check the validity of the data. Write IF statements that perform the following checks.

(a) Age must be between 21 and 65, inclusive.
(b) Number of dependents must be at least one.
(c) Marital status must be
     0 for single
     1 for divorced
     2 for married
(d) A negative age terminates the entry process.

Answer:

(a) IF A<21 OR A>65
(b) IF N<1
(c) IF M>=Ø AND M<3
(d) IF A<Ø

PROBLEM 4-21 Write a loop that computes the values of $2^1, 2^2, 2^3, \ldots, 2^{14}$ and then prints those values.

Answer:

```
1Ø REM I is Index, P is the current Power of 2
2Ø I=Ø
3Ø I2=2
4Ø P=1
5Ø I=I+1
6Ø P=P*I2
7Ø PRINT P
8Ø IF I<14 THEN 5Ø
1ØØ END
```

PROBLEM 4-22 Change the program in Problem 4-21 so that it will print $2^n - 1$.

Answer: Change line 70 to

```
7Ø PRINT P-1
```

PROBLEM 4-23 Revise the program in Problem 4-21 so that the user can enter the root and the maximum value of the exponent.

Answer:

```
1Ø PRINT "This program will print a number and all its powers"
2Ø PRINT "up to a maximum exponent that you select."
3Ø PRINT "Enter a number and the maximum exponent."
4Ø INPUT N, M
5Ø PRINT
6Ø PRINT "Exponent    Power"
7Ø I=Ø
8Ø P=N
9Ø I=I+1
1ØØ IF I>M THEN 2ØØ
11Ø PRINT "    ";I, P
12Ø P=P*N
13Ø GOTO 9Ø
2ØØ END
```

PROBLEM 4-24 Write a program that uses an IF . . . GOTO loop to print the numbers from 0 through 9, each on a separate line, skipping a line between each number.

Answer:

```
1Ø I=Ø
2Ø PRINT I
3Ø PRINT
4Ø I=I+1
5Ø IF I<=9 THEN 2Ø
6Ø END
```

PROBLEM 4-25 Write an IF . . . GOTO loop that prints the even numbers between 2 and 40 on separate lines, single spaced.

Answer:

```
1Ø I=2
2Ø PRINT I
3Ø I=I+2
4Ø IF I<=4Ø THEN 2Ø
```

PROBLEM 4-26 Write an IF . . . GOTO loop that prints the numbers from 20 through 10 on separate lines, single spaced.

Answer:

```
1Ø I=2Ø
2Ø PRINT I
3Ø I=I-1
4Ø IF I>=1Ø THEN 2Ø
```

PROBLEM 4-27 You deposit $1,000 in a savings account at 6% interest per year (0.5% per month), on January 1, 1984. Write a program that compounds the interest each month and reports the year in which the investment will reach $1,500.

Answer:

```
10 REM S is Saving, G is Goal, M is Month, Y is Year
20 S=1000
30 G=1500
40 M=1
50 Y=1984
60 M=M+1
70 S=S*1.005
80 IF S<G THEN 60
90 Y=Y+M/12
100 PRINT "Your savings account will exceed $";G; "in"; INT(Y); "."
200 END
```

Comment: This program multiplies the amount of S by 1.005 to increment it by 0.5% each month. The amount of S could be reported month by month if desired. The loop includes only lines 60, 70, and 80. Lines 20 through 50 initialize the variables. Line 90 increments the year from its initial value of 1984, but only after 12 months have passed. The function INT in line 100 removes the decimal fraction from the year, so that July, 1988, is printed as 1988, not 1988.5.

PROBLEM 4-28 The factorial of a number is the product of all integers from 1 up to and including that number. For example: $1! = 1$; $2! = 1 \times 2 = 2$; $3! = 1 \times 2 \times 3 = 6$; and so on. By definition, $0! = 1$. Write an IF . . . GOTO loop that calculates the factorial of an input number.

Answer:

```
10 REM F1 is the input value, F2 is the value of F1!, I is an Index
20 INPUT "This program computes factorials. Enter a number"; F1
30 I=0
40 F2=1
50 IF F1=0 THEN 90
60 I=I+1
70 F2=F2*I
80 IF I<F1 THEN 60
90 PRINT F1; "! ="; F2
100 END
```

If the input number is 0, the first IF statement skips the loop and branches directly to the output statement (line 90), which prints

```
0 ! = 1
```

If the input number is any number greater than 0, starting in line 60 the loop generates 1 and larger integers, multiplying each into F2 until the value of F1 is reached.

PROBLEM 4-29 Using an IF . . . GOTO loop, write a program that accepts a series of single integers as input and reports whether each number is larger than, smaller than, or the same as the previous entry. (Input is assumed to be from a terminal keyboard, and output is displayed on the terminal screen.) Allow for twenty items of input data.

Answer:

```
10 REM L is Last number, N is Next number, I is Index
20 I=0
30 INPUT "Enter a number"; L
```
(*continued*)

(*continued*)

```
40 PRINT
50 INPUT "Enter another number"; N
60 IF N>L THEN PRINT "That number is larger than the last one."
70 IF N<L THEN PRINT "That number is smaller than the last one."
80 IF N=L THEN PRINT "That number is the same as the last one."
90 I=I+1
100 L=N
110 IF I<=20 THEN 40
120 PRINT "That's all."
130 END
```

Comment: Lines 20 and 30 take care of initialization, setting the counter I to 0 and asking for the first number. After that, the program continues to loop back to line 40 from the last IF statement until I reaches 21. Within the loop, three IF statements test the three possible relationships between the two numbers. Then the counter is incremented in line 90, and the value of N is assigned to L in line 100.

PROBLEM 4-30 Assume that you want to use your computer as a thermostat to control the temperature in your house. Using IF and GOTO statements, write a program that asks for the temperature you want to maintain, the current temperature, and then tells you to turn the furnace on when the actual temperature is two degrees below the desired temperature and off when the actual temperature is two degrees above the desired temperature. (Assume that the computer is attached to a thermal sensor, which constantly monitors the temperature.)

Answer:

```
10 REM This program asks for temperature readings, compares
11 REM them to a thermostat setting, and controls the furnace.
20 I=0
30 INPUT "Please set the thermostat"; T
40 INPUT "What is the current temperature"; T1
50 REM Terminate this program if 0 is entered.
60 IF T1=0 THEN 110
70 REM Check for normal temperature fluctuation.
80 IF T1>=T+2 THEN PRINT "Turn furnace off"
90 IF T1<=T-2 THEN PRINT "Turn furnace on"
100 GOTO 40
110 END
```

Comment: This program creates an infinite loop that constantly asks for the current temperature. Some refinements could be made. There should be a provision for resetting the desired temperature and, perhaps, for changing the tolerance of plus or minus two degrees.

PROBLEM 4-31 Add the following enhancements to the program in Problem 4-30: A fire alarm routine that will warn you if the actual temperature exceeds 120°, and a furnace failure alarm that will print a message if the temperature drops 15° below the desired level.

Answer:

```
10 REM This program asks for temperature readings, compares
11 REM them to a thermostat setting, and 'controls' the furnace or
12 REM advises the user to take emergency action.
20 I=0
30 INPUT "Please set the thermostat"; T
40 INPUT "What is the current temperature"; T1
50 REM Terminate this program if 0 is entered.
```

(*continued*)

(*continued*)

```
 6Ø IF T1=Ø THEN 18Ø
 7Ø REM Check for dangerous conditions
 8Ø IF T1>12Ø THEN 15Ø
 9Ø IF T1<T-15 THEN 17Ø
1ØØ REM If there are no dangerous conditions, check for normal
11Ø REM temperature fluctuation.
12Ø IF T1>T+2 THEN PRINT "Turn furnace off"
13Ø IF T1<T-2 THEN PRINT "Turn furnace on"
14Ø GOTO 4Ø
15Ø PRINT "CALL FIRE DEPARTMENT 555-6676"
16Ø GOTO 18Ø
17Ø PRINT "Furnace broken. Call Aaron's Plumbing and Heating"
18Ø END
```

PROBLEM 4-32 In Example 4-5, we wrote a complicated IF condition that told you whether or not to put on your coat before going out:

```
2Ø IF T<45 OR (T<5Ø AND F$<>'WARM') THEN PRINT "Put on your coat."
```

Analyze the IF condition, and find the results produced by various combinations of temperature (T) and forecast (F$).

Answer: The IF condition tells you to put on your coat if the temperature is less than 45° or if the temperature is between 45° and 50° and the forecast is not for warm weather. How can you tell? Let's analyze the condition, step by step. First, you must assume that the values of T and F$ have been assigned previously in the program. T is the outside temperature, and F$ will be either 'WARM' or 'COOL.' Second, in evaluating the entire condition, you must first evaluate the expressions in parentheses. Third, two significant temperatures are given: 45° and 50°. Let's use three values for T that fall below, between, and above those cutoff temperatures; for example, 40°, 47°, and 51°. Our values for F$ are 'WARM' and 'COOL.' Let's start with 40° and WARM.

```
2Ø IF T<45   OR  (T<5Ø   AND F$<>'WARM') THEN PRINT "Put on your coat."
       TRUE OR ( TRUE AND    FALSE    )
       TRUE OR            FALSE
              TRUE
```

First, evaluate within parentheses. Substituting 40 for T in T<50 gives us a value of TRUE. F$<>'WARM' is the same as F$ = COOL, which in this case is FALSE. Now we can evaluate the condition IF . . . TRUE and FALSE, which is FALSE. Moving to the next level, we evaluate the condition on the left side of OR (TRUE) with the condition on the right side (FALSE). We know that if either side of an expression with OR is TRUE, then the entire expression is TRUE. Therefore, if the temperature is 40°, then the condition will be TRUE and you will have to put on a coat, no matter what the forecast is for the day. Now try 47° and WARM.

```
2Ø IF T<45    OR  (T<5Ø   AND F$<>'WARM') THEN PRINT "Put on your coat."
       FALSE OR ( TRUE AND    FALSE    )
       FALSE OR           FALSE
            FALSE
```

Evaluating the condition within parentheses yields a value of FALSE. This brings us to the third line, where FALSE OR FALSE is FALSE, so the entire condition is FALSE and you will not have to wear a coat. Now try 47° and COOL.

```
2Ø IF T<45    OR  (T<5Ø   AND F$<>'WARM') THEN PRINT "Put on your coat."
       FALSE OR ( TRUE AND    TRUE    )
       FALSE OR           TRUE
            TRUE
```

Here, the value of F$<>'WARM' is TRUE because our forecast is COOL. Continuing the evaluations at each level yields a value of TRUE for the entire condition. Now try 51° and COOL.

```
20 IF T<45   OR (T<50   AND F$<>'WARM') THEN PRINT "Put on your coat."
        FALSE OR ( FALSE AND   TRUE     )
        FALSE OR             FALSE
              FALSE
```

Based on the IF condition we are using, whenever T is not less than 50, both sides of the OR will be FALSE. The expression on the left side is obvious. On the right side, remember that an AND expression is FALSE if either side is FALSE, and T < 50 will always be FALSE when T is 50 or above. The result will be the same for 51° and WARM as well.

5 LOOPS

5-1. The FOR . . . NEXT Loop

Many programs perform calculations that must be repeated hundreds, thousands, even millions of times. In BASIC, this repetitive processing is accomplished by loops. Chapter 4 discussed loops constructed with IF and GOTO statements. This chapter continues the discussion of loops by introducing the FOR statement and the NEXT statement, which together define loops in BASIC.

A. The FOR statement

The FOR statement specifies the number of times that a block of lines is to be repeated. The block of lines to be repeated follows the FOR statement and constitutes the *scope*, or *range*, of the FOR statement. In the FOR statement, you specify the name of the variable to be used as a counter, its initial value, its ending value, and, optionally, the step (increment) to be added to the counter each time through the loop.

B. The general form of the FOR statement

The form of the FOR statement is

> FOR *index variable* = *starting value* TO *end value* STEP *increment*

1. The *index variable* is a variable that is used as a counter to control the number of loop repetitions. The value of the index begins with the *starting value* and is changed by the *increment* each time through the loop, until it reaches the *end value*.
2. The *starting value* is a constant or variable that specifies the initial value of the index. Typically, the starting value is 1.
3. The *end value* is the value against which the index is tested. Usually, the end value is greater than the starting value, causing the loop to "count up." When the index becomes greater than the end value, the loop terminates and control passes to the line following the NEXT statement. The end value may be less than the starting value. In this case, the increment must be negative, and the loop will "count down."
4. The step *increment* is the value that is added to the index each time through the loop. The step is optional; if omitted, its value is assumed to be 1.

C. The NEXT statement

The FOR statement is always used in conjunction with the NEXT statement. The NEXT statement ends the loop created by the FOR statement.

EXAMPLE 5-1: In the following structure, the FOR statement sets up a loop that will repeat five times. All the statements within the loop will be repeated in order, and NEXT marks the end of the repeated block.

```
10 FOR I=1 TO 5
   .
   .
   .
Lines to be repeated
   .
   .
   .
50 NEXT I
```

D. The operation of the FOR . . . NEXT loop

The statement

```
FOR I=1 TO 5
```

means "execute the lines that follow, up to and including NEXT I. For the first repetition, set I to 1. Increment I by 1 each time the lines are repeated until I is greater than 5. Then 'drop through' to the line following NEXT I." This is illustrated in Figure 5-1.

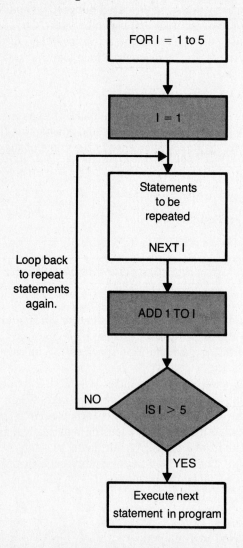

Figure 5-1

The gray boxes in the chart are actions performed as a part of the loop; they are not explicit BASIC statements but are executed as an implicit part of the FOR . . . NEXT pair.

EXAMPLE 5-2: The following program shows a simple FOR . . . NEXT loop in which a single line is repeated five times.

```
1Ø FOR I=1 TO 5
2Ø PRINT "Loop repetition:" I
3Ø NEXT I
4Ø PRINT "Loop completed."
5Ø END
```

The output of this program is

```
Loop repetition: 1
Loop repetition: 2
Loop repetition: 3
Loop repetition: 4
Loop repetition: 5
Loop completed.
```

Note that the value of I was used in the first PRINT statement in the loop. In general, you may use the index of the loop within the loop in any way you wish, but you should not change its value in the loop.

5-2. The Parameters of the FOR . . . NEXT Loop

The FOR . . . NEXT loop has four parameters that control its execution. These parameters were discussed briefly in Section 5-1; they are discussed here in detail.

1. The *index variable* is a counter that controls the number of repetitions of the loop.
2. The *starting value* is a value that is assigned to the index variable the first time through the loop.
3. The *end value* is a value that is compared to the index to determine if the loop should terminate.
4. The *step increment* is a value that is added to the index each time the loop is repeated.

The index must be a variable, since its value changes during each repetition of the loop. The other three parameters may be variables, constants, or expressions.

A. The index variable

The index variable is used as a counter. It is assigned the starting value when the FOR statement is first executed, and is modified by the value of the step each time the loop is repeated. The value of the index can be used elsewhere in the loop; however, it should not be changed within the loop through use in a READ or INPUT statement or on the left side of a LET statement.

B. The starting value

The starting value may be a constant, variable, or expression of any value. FOR . . . NEXT loops often start at 1, but another value can be used.

EXAMPLE 5-3: In the program fragment below, Y is used as a starting value to step through the years of the 20th century.

```
1Ø FOR Y=19ØØ TO 1999
 .
 .
 .
1ØØ NEXT Y
```

C. The end value

The end value may be a constant, variable, or expression. It is usually greater than the starting value, in which case the FOR loop will count up. If it is less than the starting value, a negative step should be specified and the loop will count down.

D. The step increment

The step may be a constant, variable, or expression. If the step is not specified, BASIC will set it to 1.

EXAMPLE 5-4: Programs 1 through 4 show the effect of changing the step in a loop.

```
5 REM Program 1              5 REM Program 2
10 FOR I=1 TO 10 STEP 1      10 FOR I=1 TO 10 STEP 2
20 PRINT I                   20 PRINT I
30 NEXT I                    30 NEXT I
```

Display: Display:

```
1                            1
2                            3
3                            5
4                            7
5                            9
6
7
8
9
10
```

```
5 REM Program 3              5 REM Program 4
10 FOR I=2 TO 10 STEP 2      10 FOR I=1 TO 10 STEP 3
20 PRINT I                   20 PRINT I
30 NEXT I                    30 NEXT I
```

Display: Display:

```
2                            1
4                            4
6                            7
8                            10
10
```

Compare programs 2 and 4. If the last value of I in program 2 were incremented again by 2, its value would be 11, which is more than the end value, so the loop terminates. In program 4, the last value of I equals the end value, which causes the loop to terminate.

5-3. Using the FOR . . . NEXT Loop

A. Repeating a block of lines a specified number of times

A block of lines may be repeated a specified number of times by enclosing them in a FOR . . . NEXT loop that has a starting value of 1 and an end value equal to the number of repetitions desired.

EXAMPLE 5-5: The following program executes the PRINT statements 25 times, which prints an address 25 times.

```
1Ø FOR I=1 TO 25
2Ø PRINT "ROSE'S FLOWER SHOP"
3Ø PRINT "25 GLADIOLUS DRIVE"
4Ø PRINT "SWEET PEA, NJ Ø8811"
5Ø NEXT I
```

B. Repeating a block of lines a variable number of times

A FOR . . . NEXT loop may be set up to repeat a block of lines a certain number of times as specified by the user. In this type of structure, the end value is a variable.

EXAMPLE 5-6: The following program executes the PRINT statements N times, where N is a number entered by the user.

```
1Ø INPUT N
2Ø FOR I=1 TO N
3Ø PRINT "ROSE'S FLOWER SHOP"
4Ø PRINT "25 GLADIOLUS DRIVE"
5Ø PRINT "SWEET PEA, NJ Ø8811"
6Ø NEXT I
```

C. Using the index in the loop

The index variable may be used in the loop as long as its value is not changed.

EXAMPLE 5-7: In the following program, the index I varies from L to M, two values input by the user. The square root of I is computed and a table of square roots starting with L and ending with M is printed.

```
1Ø INPUT "ENTER START AND END VALUES"; L, M
2Ø FOR I=L TO M
3Ø S=SQR(I)
4Ø PRINT I, S
5Ø NEXT I
6Ø END
```

D. Summing a set of numbers

One of the most important and frequently used procedures in BASIC programming is summing a series of values. The FOR . . . NEXT loop is a simple yet efficient method of doing this.

EXAMPLE 5-8: The following program computes the sum of N numbers, which are input as data. The sum is accumulated in variable S, which is set to an initial value of 0 outide the loop.

```
1Ø REM N is Number of values, V is individual Value
15 REM S is Sum of values
2Ø INPUT "How many values"; N
3Ø S=Ø
4Ø FOR I=1 TO N
5Ø INPUT "Value"; V
6Ø S=S+V
7Ø NEXT I
8Ø PRINT "The sum of the"; N; "numbers is"; S
9Ø END
```

E. Computing the product of a set of numbers

Another commonly used procedure in BASIC programming is computing the product of a set of numbers. Again, this is easily accomplished by using the FOR . . . NEXT loop.

EXAMPLE 5-9: We can modify the program in Example 5-8 so that it will compute the product of a set of numbers. The major change is that we use the variable P, which is initialized to 1; if it were initialized to 0, the product would be 0.

```
10 REM N is the Number of values, V is the individual Value
15 REM P is Product
20 INPUT "Number of values"; N
30 P=1
40 FOR I=1 TO N
50 INPUT "Value"; V
60 P=P*V
70 NEXT I
80 PRINT "The product of the"; N; "numbers is"; P
90 END
```

5-4. Nested Loops

A. A *nested loop* is a loop that is enclosed within another loop.

A FOR . . . NEXT loop may be placed within the range of another FOR . . . NEXT loop. In a large program, there is practically no limit to the number and type of statements that may appear within the range of a FOR . . . NEXT loop. An entire program can be enclosed within a loop if necessary.

EXAMPLE 5-10: The following program has a nested loop in lines 20 through 40. The PRINT statement in the nested loop prints the index values of both loops.

```
10 FOR I=1 TO 3
20    FOR J=1 TO 3
30        PRINT "The value of I is"; I; ". The value of J is"; J; "."
40    NEXT J
50 NEXT I
60 END
```

Display:

```
The value of I is 1 . The value of J is 1 .
The value of I is 1 . The value of J is 2 .
The value of I is 1 . The value of J is 3 .
The value of I is 2 . The value of J is 1 .
The value of I is 2 . The value of J is 2 .
The value of I is 2 . The value of J is 3 .
The value of I is 3 . The value of J is 1 .
The value of I is 3 . The value of J is 2 .
The value of I is 3 . The value of J is 3 .
```

As this output shows, the inner loop is executed entirely for each repetition of the outer loop.

EXAMPLE 5-11: The following program prints a seating chart for a classroom. The classroom has six rows, numbered from front to rear, and eight seats in each row, numbered from left to right.

```
10 REM R is Row, S is Seat
20 PRINT "ROW"
```

(continued)

(continued)

```
30 FOR R=6 TO 1 STEP -1
40    PRINT R; "> ";
50    FOR S=1 TO 8
60       PRINT S;
70    NEXT S
80    PRINT
90 NEXT R
100 PRINT
110 PRINT "              FRONT"
120 END
```

Display:

```
ROW
 6 >   1   2   3   4   5   6   7   8
 5 >   1   2   3   4   5   6   7   8
 4 >   1   2   3   4   5   6   7   8
 3 >   1   2   3   4   5   6   7   8
 2 >   1   2   3   4   5   6   7   8
 1 >   1   2   3   4   5   6   7   8

                FRONT
```

In this program, an inner loop (terminating at line 70) is nested within another loop (terminating at line 90). The inner loop is indented so that it will be easier to identify as a loop; the spaces have no effect on the execution of the program. During each iteration of the outer loop, the index R is printed as a row number, and then the inner loop executes eight times; its index, S, is used to print the seat numbers in the row.

B. Guidelines for using nested loops

    1. A FOR . . . NEXT loop should always be entered through the "top." Otherwise the index will not be defined.

EXAMPLE 5-12: In the following program the loops cross each other. Consequently, the program will not work and will produce an error message.

```
┌─ 20 FOR I=1 TO 10
│     .
│     .
│     .
│┌─ 40    FOR J=1 TO 5
││     .
││     .
││     .
└│─ 60 NEXT I
 │     .
 │     .
 │     .
 └─ 80    NEXT J
```

Looking at this tangle of FOR and NEXT statements, it is hard to understand what is actually intended. This type of problem is common in longer programs, where FOR and NEXT statements are often separated by many other statements.

    2. IF and GOTO statements may be used to branch out of a nested FOR . . . NEXT loop. In fact, in nested loops, the branch may transfer control out of several loops at the same time.

However, as with any other FOR . . . NEXT structure, you cannot transfer control *into* a loop.

3. More than one loop may be terminated at the same NEXT statement. Some BASIC interpreters do not require an index variable in the NEXT statement. If there is no variable, the NEXT statement is matched with the last FOR statement that has not been executed. This means that several loops may terminate at the same NEXT statement. However, this practice is not recommended.

5-5. Valid and Invalid Loop Structures

Certain nestings of loops and transfers of control are not permitted in BASIC.

A. Crossed loops

Crossed loops will not work in BASIC. For example:

```
 ┌─ 1Ø  FOR  I=1  TO  2Ø
┌┼─ 2Ø  FOR  J=1  TO  5
││      .
││      .                                INVALID
││      .
││      .
│└─ 8Ø  NEXT  I
└── 9Ø  NEXT  J
```

Neither loop is properly nested within the other, and it is difficult to determine what is to be done.

B. Transfers into a loop

Transfers of control into a loop bypassing the FOR statement are invalid, because an initial value for the loop index has not been established.

```
 ┌─ 3Ø  GOTO  6Ø
┌┼─ 4Ø  FOR  K=1  TO  N
││      .
││      .
││      .                                INVALID
│└─ 6Ø  . . .
│       .
│       .
└── 8Ø  NEXT  K
```

C. Transfers with nested loops

The restrictions on transfers of control within nested loops can be summarized in two diagrams. The first shows valid transfers of control.

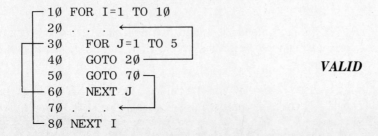

```
 ┌─ 1Ø  FOR  I=1  TO  1Ø
 │  2Ø  . . .  ◄────────┐
┌┼─ 3Ø      FOR  J=1  TO  5
││  4Ø      GOTO  2Ø ───┘
││  5Ø      GOTO  7Ø ┐            VALID
│└─ 6Ø      NEXT  J  │
│   7Ø  . . .  ◄─────┘
└── 8Ø  NEXT  I
```

The second shows invalid transfers of control.

```
┌─ 1Ø  FOR  I=1  TO  1Ø
│  2Ø  GOTO  4Ø ─────────┐
│┌─ 3Ø      FOR  J=1  TO  5 ┐
││  4Ø       . . .    ←─────┘
││  5Ø       . . .    ←─────┐
│└─ 6Ø      NEXT  J         │
│   7Ø  GOTO  5Ø ───────────┘
└─ 8Ø  NEXT  I
```

INVALID

D. Entry from the top

A FOR . . . NEXT loop should always be entered from the top.

```
┌─ invalid entry
│┌─ valid entry
│└→ FOR  I=1  TO  1Ø
│      .
│      .
│      .
└────→ NEXT  I
```

If this restriction were not observed, the FOR . . . NEXT loop would not be properly initialized. It is valid, however, to transfer out of a FOR . . . NEXT loop before its normal end.

RAISE YOUR GRADES

Can you explain . . . ?

☑ the purpose of the FOR statement
☑ the form of the FOR statement
☑ the relationship of the NEXT statement to the FOR statement
☑ how the FOR . . . NEXT loop operates
☑ the four parameters of the FOR . . . NEXT loop
☑ how nested loops operate
☑ some valid and invalid loop structures

SUMMARY

1. The FOR . . . NEXT loop executes a series of lines a set number of times, under control of the program.
2. In writing the FOR statement, you specify an *index* variable, *starting* and *end values*, and (optionally) the *step* by which the index is to be increased during each repetition of the loop.
3. The index of the FOR . . . NEXT loop may be any variable. The starting value, end value, and step may be constants, variables, or expressions.
4. A negative step may be used, so that the loop "counts down" from the starting value to the end value.
5. Each iteration of a FOR . . . NEXT loop updates the value of the index variable. The value of the index may be used elsewhere in the loop, but it may not be changed. The index variable may be used for any purpose elsewhere in the program.
6. FOR . . . NEXT loops should be entered through the FOR statement (from the top) in order to properly initialize the loop. However, control may be transferred out of the loop by IF statements before the loop would normally terminate.

7. Any statement may appear within the range of a FOR . . . NEXT loop, and there is no limit on the length of the range. Often, another FOR . . . NEXT loop is executed within the range of an outer loop; this is called a nested loop. Any reasonable number of loops may be nested, but the complexities of the resulting logic require careful programming.

RAPID REVIEW   Answers

True or False?

1. If the programmer does not supply a value for the step increment, BASIC will set the increment to zero.   False

2. The index variable of a FOR . . . NEXT loop can be defined and then used elsewhere in the program.   True

3. The index variable will always assume the end value during the last iteration of the loop.   False

4. The last line in a FOR . . . NEXT loop must be a LET statement.   False

5. A FOR . . . NEXT loop can start at zero.   True

6. Two separate FOR . . . NEXT loops can be nested within the range of an outer loop.   True

7. FOR I = 2500 TO 5000 STEP 2000 is a valid FOR statement.   True

Fill in the blanks

1. FOR I=2 TO 10 STEP 2 starts a loop that will execute _____ times.   five

2. The _____ is a constant or variable that specifies the first value of a loop index.   starting value

3. The _____ is a value that is added to the index each time the loop is repeated.   step

4. A _____ is a loop that is enclosed within another loop.   nested loop

5. The statements that are to be repeated in a FOR . . . NEXT loop constitute the _____ of the FOR statement.   range, or scope

SOLVED PROBLEMS

PROBLEM 5-1 Identify the correct and incorrect FOR . . . NEXT loop structures.

(a)   FOR I=1 TO 12
        .
        .
        .
    6Ø NEXT I

(b) 2Ø FOR I=1 TO 1Ø
        .
        .
        .
    8Ø NEXT I

(c) 3Ø GOTO 7Ø
         .
         .
         .
     5Ø FOR I=1 TO 1Ø
         .
         .
         .
     7Ø   S=S+1
     1ØØ NEXT I

(d) 2Ø FOR I=1 TO 15
         .
         .
         .
     4Ø   GOTO 5Ø
         .
         .
         .
     5Ø NEXT I

(e) 4Ø FOR I=1 TO 5
         .
         .
         .
     5Ø   IF A>1ØØ GOTO 6Ø
         .
         .
         .
     6Ø NEXT I

Answers:

(a) Incorrect. The FOR statement must have a line number.

(b) Correct.

(c) Incorrect. The GOTO statement transfers control into the FOR . . . NEXT loop, which is not allowed because the index is not defined unless the FOR statement is executed.

(d) Correct.

(e) Correct. The IF statement skips the last part of the loop and then continues with more repetitions by transferring control to the NEXT statement.

PROBLEM 5-2 Identify the correct and incorrect FOR statements and loop structures.

(a) 1Ø FOR I=1 TO 1Ø
     2Ø FOR I=1 TO 1Ø
         .
         .
         .
     6Ø NEXT I
     7Ø NEXT I

(b) 1Ø FOR I=1 TO 2Ø
     2Ø FOR J=61 TO 68 STEP 3
         .
         .
         .
     1ØØ NEXT J
     11Ø NEXT I

(c) 10 FOR I=F TO E STEP S
.
.
.
   80 NEXT I

(d) 10 FOR P=6 TO 3

(e) 10 FOR A=1 TO 100
   20 FOR B=1 TO 50
.
.
.
   40 NEXT B
   50 FOR D=1 TO 10
.
.
.
   80 NEXT D
   100 NEXT A

(f) 20 FOR X=10 TO 0 STEP -3.2

Answers:

(a) Incorrect. Two loops cannot have the same index at the same time. If the index is incremented by one loop, the other loop will be thrown off.
(b) Correct.
(c) Correct, as long as permissible values have been assigned to the three variables F, E, and S.
(d) Incorrect. If the end value of the loop is less than the starting value, a negative increment must be specified; for example, 10 FOR P=6 TO 3 STEP −1.
(e) Correct.
(f) Correct.

PROBLEM 5-3 Identify the correct and incorrect FOR statements.

(a) FOR I=1 TO 3 STEP 2
(b) FOR A=B TO C STEP D
(c) FOR 2=1.3 TO 7.0
(d) FOR J=13 TO 2 STEP -1
(e) FOR P=-2.3 TO 12.9 STEP -3.
(f) FOR X=1 TO LIMIT STEP 2
(g) FOR B=1 TO 20 STEP 0

Answers:

(a) Correct.
(b) Correct if the variables are assigned permissible values.
(c) Incorrect. The index must be a variable.
(d) Correct.
(e) Incorrect. The increment must be positive because the end value is greater than the beginning value. On the other hand, if the increment is negative, the end value must be less than the beginning value.
(f) Correct if the variable LIMIT is assigned a permissible value.
(g) Incorrect. An increment of 0 is not permitted, because this would create an infinite loop.

PROBLEM 5-4 What values will this FOR statement generate?

   FOR I=1 TO 10

Answer: 1, 2, 3, 4, 5, 6, 7, 8, 9, 10

PROBLEM 5-5 What values will this FOR statement generate?

```
FOR I=1 TO 2
```

Answer: 1, 2

PROBLEM 5-6 Write a FOR . . . NEXT loop that will print the numbers from 0 to 9 on separate lines, skipping two lines each time.

Answer:

```
1Ø FOR I=Ø to 9
2Ø    PRINT I
3Ø    PRINT
4Ø    PRINT
5Ø NEXT I
6Ø END
```

PROBLEM 5-7 Write a FOR . . . NEXT loop that will print the numbers from 40 to 20 on successive lines.

Answer:

```
1Ø FOR N=4Ø TO 2Ø STEP -1
2Ø    PRINT N
3Ø NEXT N
4Ø END
```

PROBLEM 5-8 What values will this FOR statement generate?

```
FOR I=1 TO 1Ø STEP 2
```

Answer: 1, 3, 5, 7, 9

PROBLEM 5-9 What values will this FOR statement generate?

```
FOR I=1 TO 11 STEP 2
```

Answer: 1, 3, 5, 7, 9, 11

PROBLEM 5-10 Write a FOR . . . NEXT loop that will compute R^N using multiplication, and will repeat the procedure ten times, reading a new value of R and N each time.

Answer:

```
2Ø FOR T=1 TO 1Ø
3Ø    INPUT "Number"; R
4Ø    INPUT "Exponent"; N
5Ø    P=1
6Ø    IF N=Ø THEN 1ØØ
7Ø    FOR J=1 TO N
8Ø       P=P*R
9Ø    NEXT J
1ØØ    PRINT R; "to the power of"; N; "is"; P
11Ø NEXT T
12Ø END
```

Comment: This program calculates R^N by performing successive multiplications. However, if the value of N is 0, line 60 skips directly to the output statement in line 100. (Any number to the power of 0 is 1.) Otherwise, the loop in lines 70–90 is executed. If N = 1, this loop will be executed once. The purpose of the loop with the index T is to repeat the program ten times.

PROBLEM 5-11 Write a FOR . . . NEXT loop that will compute factorials. The factorial of a given number is the product of all integers from one up to and including the number. The factorial of five is written 5! and equals $1 \times 2 \times 3 \times 4 \times 5 = 120$. By definition, 0! = 1, and 1! = 1.

Answer:

```
20 REM This program computes a factorial.
30 INPUT F1
40 F2=1
50 IF F1=0 THEN 90
60 FOR I=1 TO F1
70    F2=F2*I
80 NEXT I
90 PRINT F1; "! is equal to "; F2
100 END
```

PROBLEM 5-12 What values will this FOR statement generate?

```
FOR I=10 TO 5 STEP -1
```

Answer: 10, 9, 8, 7, 6, 5

PROBLEM 5-13 Write a FOR . . . NEXT loop that will sum all numbers from 1 to 50 that are not multiples of 4.

Answer:

```
10 REM This program sums all numbers from 1 to 50 that are
11 REM not multiples of 4.
12 REM S is Sum
20 S=0
30 FOR I=1 TO 50 STEP 4
40    FOR J=I TO I+2
50       IF J>50 THEN 100
60          S=S+J
70    NEXT J
80 NEXT I
100 PRINT "The sum of all numbers from 1 to 50"
110 PRINT "that are not multiples of 4 is"; S
120 END
```

Comment: The key to this program is in line 30 and line 40. J assumes the values 1, 2, 3, 5, 6, 7, 9, . . . because it always starts from one more than a multiple of 4, as determined by the step in line 30.

PROBLEM 5-14 Modify the program in Problem 5-13 so that the user can enter the value of the number whose multiples are to be skipped and the upper limit of the numbers to be summed.

Answer:

```
20 PRINT "This program prints the sum of all numbers"
21 PRINT "up to and including a limit (which you specify)"
22 PRINT "that are not multiples of a number that you specify."
30 INPUT "Number"; N
```

(continued)

(*continued*)

```
40 INPUT "Limit"; L
50 S=0
60 FOR I=1 TO L STEP N
70    FOR J=I TO I+N-2
80       IF J>L THEN 120
90       S=S+J
100   NEXT J
110 NEXT I
120 PRINT "The sum of all numbers from 1 to"; L
130 PRINT "that are not multiples of"; N; "is"; S
200 END
```

Comment: This program reads the multiple that is to be skipped in the summing procedure, and uses that multiple as the step in the outside FOR . . . NEXT loop. Since the loop index starts at 1, each successive value of the index will be one more than each successive multiple. For example, if the multiples are 7, 14, 21, . . . , the index values will be 1, 8, 15, 22, ... These index values are used each time as the starting value of the inner loop, and the end value is one less than the next multiple $(I+N-2)$, so that the multiples are never generated in the inner loop and cannot be summed. When the inner loop generates the value of L in line 80, the whole procedure terminates, and lines 120 and 130 print the output.

PROBLEM 5-15 What values will this FOR statement generate?

```
FOR I=-1.3 TO 9.7 STEP 1.2
```

Answer: $-1.3, -0.1, 1.1, 2.3, 3.5, 4.7, 5.9, 7.1, 8.3, 9.5$

PROBLEM 5-16 What values will this FOR statement generate?

```
FOR I=1.3 TO 0.6 STEP -0.2
```

Answer: 1.3, 1.1, 0.9, 0.7

PROBLEM 5-17 Write a FOR . . . NEXT loop that counts backward from 100 to 4 by threes.

Answer:

```
20 FOR I=100 TO 4 STEP -3
30    PRINT I
40 NEXT I
50 END
```

PROBLEM 5-18 Write a program that converts miles to kilometers, ranging from 1 to 50 miles, and then prints a table that displays the results of these conversions. (One mile = 1.609 kilometers.)

Answer:

```
20 PRINT "MILES       KILOMETERS"
30 PRINT
40 FOR M=1 TO 50
50    PRINT M, M*1.609
60 NEXT M
70 END
```

Display:

MILES	KILOMETERS
1	1.6
2	3.2
.	.
.	.
.	.
5Ø	8Ø.5

PROBLEM 5-19 Write a program that converts kilometers to miles, ranging from 5 to 250 kilometers by fives, and then prints a table that displays the results of these conversions.

Answer:

```
2Ø PRINT "KILOMETERS   MILES"
3Ø PRINT
4Ø FOR K=5 TO 25Ø STEP 5
5Ø    PRINT K, K/1.6Ø9
6Ø NEXT K
7Ø END
```

Display:

KILOMETERS	MILES
5	3.1
1Ø	6.2
.	.
.	.
.	.
25Ø	155.4

PROBLEM 5-20 What values will be generated for I by the following FOR statements?

```
1Ø FOR J=I TO 3
2Ø    FOR I=1 TO 3
```

Answer: 1, 2, 3, 1, 2, 3, 1, 2, 3

PROBLEM 5-21 What values will be generated for I by the following loop?

```
1Ø FOR J=1Ø TO 3Ø STEP 1Ø
2Ø    FOR I=J TO J+3
3Ø    NEXT I
4Ø    FOR I=J+9 TO J+11
5Ø    NEXT I
6Ø NEXT J
```

Answer: 10, 11, 12, 13, 19, 20, 21, 20, 21, 22, 23, 29, 30, 31, 30, 31, 32, 33, 39, 40, 41

PROBLEM 5-22 You borrow $500 at an interest rate of 10% per week. Write a program that will compute and print what you owe if you keep the money for 1 week, 2 weeks, . . . , 10 weeks.

Answer:

```
2Ø L=5ØØ
3Ø I=.1
```

(*continued*)

(continued)

```
40  PRINT "AT END OF WEEK   YOU OWE"
50  PRINT
60  FOR W=1 TO 10
70     L=L*(1+I)
80     PRINT "    "; W; "            "; L
90  NEXT W
100 END
```

Display:

```
AT END OF WEEK    YOU OWE

    1             550.00
    2             605.00
    .                .
    .                .
    .                .
   10             1296.87
```

PROBLEM 5-23 Modify the program in Problem 5-22 so that it allows the user to enter the amount of the loan and then computes and prints out the amounts owed at interest rates of 10%, 20%, ... , 100%.

Answer:

```
30   INPUT "Amount of loan"; L
40   FOR J=10 TO 100 STEP 10
50      I=J/100
60      PRINT "PAYMENT ON A LOAN OF $"; L; "AT"; J; "% PER WEEK:"
70      PRINT "AT END OF WEEK   YOU OWE"
80      PRINT
90      L1=L
100     FOR K=1 TO 10
110        L1=L1*(1+I)
120        PRINT "        "; K; "        $"; L1
130     NEXT K
140     PRINT
150     PRINT
160  NEXT J
170  END
```

Display:

```
PAYMENT ON A LOAN OF $ 500 AT 10 % PER WEEK:
AT END OF WEEK   YOU OWE

    1           $ 550
    .             .
    .             .
    .             .
```

PROBLEM 5-24 Write a program that will print the days of the years 1983 and 1984 in the form month/day/year—for example, 12/25/83—one day per line.

Answer:

```
10   REM Y is Year, M is Month, D is Day, D1 is length of month
20   FOR Y=83 TO 84
30      FOR M=1 TO 12
40         D1=31
50            IF M=4 OR M=6 OR M=9 OR M=11 THEN D1=30
60            IF M=2                       THEN D1=28
70            IF M=2 AND Y=84              THEN D1=29
80         FOR D=1 TO D1
90            PRINT M; "/"; D; "/"; Y
100        NEXT D
110     NEXT M
120 NEXT Y
130 END
```

Display:

```
1 / 1 / 83
1 / 2 / 83
.
.
.
2 / 29 / 84
.
.
.
12 / 31 / 84
```

PROBLEM 5-25 For large-quantity sales, Bugbit Computer Corp. charges $99.95 each for the first ten microcomputers ordered, $89.95 each for the next ten units ordered, and $79.95 each for all additional units. Write a program that will print a price list giving the total price for purchases of any number of computers from 1 to 40.

Answer:

```
10 REM N is Number of units, T is Total price
20 PRINT "NUMBER OF UNITS     TOTAL PRICE"
21 PRINT
30 T=0
40 FOR N=1 TO 10
50    T=T+99.95
60    PRINT N, T
70 NEXT N
80 FOR N=11 TO 20
90    T=T+89.95
100 PRINT N, T
110 NEXT N
120 FOR N=21 TO 40
130    T=T+79.95
140    PRINT N, T
150 NEXT N
160 END
```

Display:

```
NUMBER OF UNITS    TOTAL PRICE

     1                99.95
     2               199.90
     .                  .
     .                  .
     .                  .
    40              3498.00
```

PROBLEM 5-26 Write a FOR . . . NEXT loop that will generate 12 numbers of the Fibonacci series, given the first two numbers. (In the Fibonacci series, each term is the sum of the preceding two terms: 1, 1, 2, 3, 5, 8, 13, . . .)

Answer:

```
10 REM L is the Last number in the series, N is the New number
11 REM N1 is the Next number
20 L=1
30 N=1
40 PRINT L
50 PRINT N
60 FOR F=3 TO 12
70    N1=N+L
80    PRINT N1
90    L=N
100   N=N1
110 NEXT F
120 END
```

Display:

```
1
1
2
3
5
8
13
21
34
55
89
144
```

Comment: In this program, the index of the FOR . . . NEXT loop is not used for computation, but is used instead to count off ten repetitions.

PROBLEM 5-27 Write a program with three nested FOR . . . NEXT loops that prints the indices of all three loops and also prints the cumulative number of repetitions.

Answer:

```
20 PRINT "REPETITION     I          J          K"
30 PRINT "---------------------------------------------"
40 C=0
50 FOR I=1 TO 3
```

(continued)

(continued)

```
60    FOR J=1 TO 2
70        FOR K=1 TO 2
80            C=C+1
90            PRINT C, I, J, K
100       NEXT K
110     NEXT J
120 NEXT I
130 PRINT
140 PRINT "The innermost loop was executed"; C; "times."
150 END
```

Display:

```
REPETITION       I              J              K
-----------------------------------------------
    1            1              1              1
    2            1              1              2
    3            1              2              1
    4            1              2              2
    5            2              1              1
    6            2              1              2
    7            2              2              1
    8            2              2              2
    9            3              1              1
   10            3              1              2
   11            3              2              1
   12            3              2              2
```

```
The innermost loop was executed 12 times.
```

Comments:

1. C is initialized to zero before any of the loops start. Then it is incremented within the innermost loop; because of this, it must show the number of times that loop was executed. Although the loop indices will be undefined after the loop terminates, C is a separate variable and will retain its value.
2. Look closely at the way the loop indices change in the output. K changes most rapidly, because its value is generated in the innermost loop. A repetition of J is not finished until the K loop terminates, and a repetition of I is not finished until the J loop is completed. Thus, I changes most slowly.

PROBLEM 5-28 Write a program with four nested FOR . . . NEXT loops that generates the binary numbers 0000 to 1111 (0 to 15 in decimal form) and then prints the decimal number and its binary equivalent on each line.

Answer:

```
20 C=0
30 FOR B3=0 TO 1
40     FOR B2=0 TO 1
50         FOR B1=0 TO 1
60             FOR B0=0 TO 1
70                 PRINT C; "   "; B3; B2; B1; B0
80                 C=C+1
90             NEXT B0
100        NEXT B1
110    NEXT B2
120 NEXT B3
130 END
```

Display:

```
0      0 0 0 0
1      0 0 0 1
2      0 0 1 0
3      0 0 1 1
4      0 1 0 0
5      0 1 0 1
6      0 1 1 0
7      0 1 1 1
8      1 0 0 0
9      1 0 0 1
10     1 0 1 0
11     1 0 1 1
12     1 1 0 0
13     1 1 0 1
14     1 1 1 0
15     1 1 1 1
```

Comments:

1. Notice how the converted loop indices change in the column of displayed binary numbers. The rightmost digit of each binary number is the index of the innermost loop, and it changes most rapidly. The leftmost digit of each binary number is the index of the outermost loop, and it changes most slowly.
2. Incrementing C after it is printed rather than before generates values from 0 to 15.

PROBLEM 5-29 Write a program that generates the octal (base 8) numbers from 0 to 17 and then prints these numbers with their decimal equivalents (0 to 15).

Answer:

```
20 C=0
30 FOR O1=0 TO 1
40    FOR O0=0 TO 7
50       PRINT C; "    "; O1; O0
60       C=C+1
70    NEXT O0
80 NEXT O1
```

Display:

```
0      0 0
1      0 1
2      0 2
3      0 3
4      0 4
5      0 5
6      0 6
7      0 7
8      1 0
9      1 1
10     1 2
11     1 3
12     1 4
13     1 5
14     1 6
15     1 7
```

PROBLEM 5-30 Write a program that will print a sine wave.

Answer:

```
2Ø FOR I=Ø TO 1ØØ STEP .5
3Ø    FOR J=1 TO 2Ø*(SIN(I)+1)
4Ø       PRINT " ";
5Ø    NEXT J
55 PRINT "*"
6Ø NEXT I
1ØØ END
```

Display (first 20 repetitions):

```
                             *
                                   *
                                      *
                                        *
                                       *
                                  *
                             *
                       *
                    *
                   *
                   *
                     *
                          *
                              *
                                 *
                                   *
                                    *
                                  *
                              *
                        *
```

Comment: The SIN function in BASIC assumes that its argument is in radians (there are 2 pi radians in 360 degrees, or 57+ degrees in one radian). In this program, the index I of the FOR . . . NEXT loop is used as the argument in the SIN function [SIN(I)]. With a step of .5, the value of the sine is calculated about 12 times for each 360 degrees. Adding 1 to the sine moves the left side of the curve over one column, and multiplying by 20 gives the curve its proportions. Notice that BASIC calculates the value of the trigonometric function so that it can be used as a parameter in a FOR . . . NEXT loop. The inner loop just generates blanks, so that the asterisk will be printed in the right position on the line.

PROBLEM 5-31 Write a program that will print the following design for the cover of a market research report:

```
MARKET RESEARCH REPORT
   MARKET RESEARCH REPORT
      MARKET RESEARCH REPORT
         MARKET RESEARCH REPORT
            MARKET RESEARCH REPORT
         MARKET RESEARCH REPORT
      MARKET RESEARCH REPORT
   MARKET RESEARCH REPORT
MARKET RESEARCH REPORT
```

Answer:

```
20 FOR I=1 TO 4
30    FOR J=1 TO I
40       PRINT "   ";
50    NEXT J
60    PRINT "MARKET RESEARCH REPORT"
70 NEXT I
80 FOR I=5 TO 1 STEP -1
90    FOR J=1 TO I
100      PRINT "   ";
110   NEXT J
120   PRINT "MARKET RESEARCH REPORT"
130 NEXT I
140 END
```

Comment: In the first half of the program, the inside FOR . . . NEXT loop adds an extra three spaces to the beginning of the line with each repetition. In the second half of the program, the inside FOR . . . NEXT loop removes three spaces. The actions of these two loops give the design its shape.

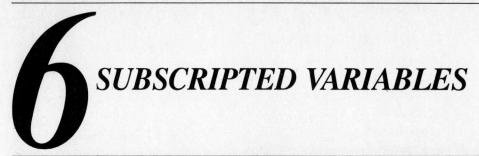

6 SUBSCRIPTED VARIABLES

6-1. Arrays

The variables we have discussed thus far are individual variables that hold one value at a time. However, it is often convenient to group several values under a single variable name. For example, the average daily temperatures for the year might be grouped under the variable D, as follows: $D(1) = 30.0$, $D(2) = 35.2$, $D(3) = 39.8$, $D(4) = 32.1$, ..., $D(364) = 30.1$, $D(365) = 32.2$. If $D(1)$ were January 1, $D(2)$ would be January 2, $D(364)$ would be December 30, and $D(365)$ would be December 31. D is called an *array variable*, and holds a collection of values. A particular element of the array is referenced by its *subscript*, which designates the element's position in the array; for example, $D(15)$ is the fifteenth value in array D. The subscript may be a variable, such as $D(I)$, or even an expression, such as $D(30*M + W*7 + D1)$.

A. An array is a collection of values.

Arrays are also called *vectors*, while the simple one-element variables are sometimes called *scalar variables*. Arrays are named in the same way as simple variables; that is, with a single letter or a letter and a number. Arrays can also be string variables, such as $D\$(30)$.

1. An array is made up of *elements*. Each element functions like a simple variable. A value can be stored in the element by an assignment or INPUT statement. The value can then be written out or used anywhere a simple variable can be used.

2. Each element is identified by a subscript, which may be a numeric constant, variable, or expression.

EXAMPLE 6-1: An array can be visualized as a row of numbered boxes, each box holding a value. The row has one name, the array name, but each box has its own number, the subscript. Thus, any single box can be referenced by its name and number, and the entire row can be referenced one box at a time by calling the variable name and generating the appropriate series of numbers. The following program fragment assigns four values (7.3, 8.6, 2.1, 3.4) to the four elements in array A. The last line of the program assigns one value (9.2) to the scalar variable S. Notice how the array differs in form from the simple scalar variable. The boxes show the locations of the values after they have been assigned.

```
10 A(1)=7.3
20 A(2)=8.6
30 A(3)=2.1
40 A(4)=3.4
50 S=9.2
```

```
      A(1)   A(2)   A(3)   A(4)
   ┌──────┬──────┬──────┬──────┐        ┌──────┐
 A │ 7.3  │ 8.6  │ 2.1  │ 3.4  │     S  │ 9.2  │
   └──────┴──────┴──────┴──────┘        └──────┘
```

B. Arrays are often processed by FOR . . . NEXT loops.

It is easy to sum the values of an array by using the FOR . . . NEXT index variable as the subscript. In the following routine, S is initially set to zero. The index variable I is used as the subscript for array A. At each repetition of the loop, the next element (I) of array A is added to S. The loop terminates when all elements of A have been added to S.

```
10 N=4
20 S=Ø.Ø
30 FOR I=1 TO N
40    S=S+A(I)
50 NEXT I
```

Suppose we had used scalar variables instead of an array in this routine. The assignment of values to the four variables would be much the same.

```
A1=7.3
A2=8.6
A3=2.1
A4=3.4
```

```
    A1         A2         A3         A4
 ┌───────┐  ┌───────┐  ┌───────┐  ┌───────┐
 │       │  │       │  │       │  │       │
 │  7.3  │  │  8.6  │  │  2.1  │  │  3.4  │
 │       │  │       │  │       │  │       │
 └───────┘  └───────┘  └───────┘  └───────┘
```

However, the summation would require a large assignment statement:

```
S=A1+A2+A3+A4
```

Such an assignment statement would be acceptable for four values, but inconvenient for 20 values and impossible for 10,000 values. In addition, an assignment statement with scalar variables always sums the same number of values, while the FOR . . . NEXT loop can sum an array of any length by simply altering the end value of the loop. In the loop we just used, changing the value of N would alter the number of values summed.

EXAMPLE 6-2: Using a FOR . . . NEXT loop you can set an entire array to zero or to any other value.

```
10 N=4
20 FOR I=1 TO N
30    A(I)=Ø.Ø
40 NEXT I
```

```
      (1)    (2)    (3)    (4)
   ┌──────┬──────┬──────┬──────┐
 A │ Ø.Ø  │ Ø.Ø  │ Ø.Ø  │ Ø.Ø  │
   └──────┴──────┴──────┴──────┘
```

With each repetition of the loop, the element of array A, as specified by the value of subscript I, is set to zero. Such loops can initialize arrays of any length by altering the end value of the FOR . . . NEXT loop.

6-2. The DIM Statement

Each array element occupies the same amount of memory as a scalar variable. Thus, the array S1(1000), for example, occupies as much memory as one thousand scalar variables. BASIC automatically allocates memory space for scalar variables as they appear in the program. However, the large blocks of memory needed for arrays must be reserved at the beginning of the program. This is accomplished with a DIM statement.

A. The DIM statement allocates memory space for arrays.

The DIM (for DIMension) statement instructs the compiler or interpreter to set aside a certain amount of memory space for an array. The DIM statement must appear at the beginning of the program and may allocate space for several arrays.

B. The form of the DIM statement

The DIM statement consists of the word DIM followed by one or more array names with the desired number of elements enclosed in parentheses. The form of the DIM statement is

> DIM *array name (subscript), array name (subscript), . . .*

Two examples are

```
15 DIM A(4)
25 DIM N(1ØØØ), X(486), E$(5Ø)
```

These two statements declare arrays with 5, 1001, 487, and 51 elements, respectively. That's because the DIM statement shows the highest subscript of the array variable, not the number of elements. Array A, therefore, includes the elements A(0), A(1), A(2), A(3), and A(4).

1. When an array appears in a program, BASIC automatically allocates space for eleven array elements without using a DIM statement. This is fine as long as the array contains eleven or fewer elements. However, if the array contains more than eleven elements, a DIM statement must be used.

EXAMPLE 6-3: The following two programs are equivalent, even though the first program contains a DIM statement and the second program doesn't.

```
1Ø DIM A(1Ø)        1Ø FOR K=Ø TO 1Ø
2Ø FOR K=Ø TO 1Ø    2Ø     LET A(K)=K
3Ø     LET A(K)=K   3Ø NEXT K
4Ø NEXT K           4Ø END
5Ø END
```

The programs are equivalent because array A contains eleven elements, making the DIM statement unnecessary.

2. Even though a DIM statement is not necessary for arrays with eleven or fewer elements, it is good programming practice to always use a DIM statement to allocate space for an array. For example, if you do not use a DIM statement to allocate space for an array A(4), BASIC will automatically allocate eleven spaces, even though only five spaces are needed. This is a waste of memory.

C. An array may be dimensioned only once in a program.

As we have just discussed, an array may be dimensioned automatically or in a DIM statement. However, in most versions of BASIC an array may be dimensioned only once in a program. An array that is dimensioned twice will be invalid, even if both dimensions are the same.

1. An array will be invalid if it is first dimensioned automatically and then dimensioned again in a DIM statement.

EXAMPLE 6-4: In the following program fragment, array B7 is invalid because it is dimensioned automatically in line 20 and then dimensioned again in the DIM statement in line 40.

```
10 FOR I=1 TO 5
20    B7(I)=0
30 NEXT I
40 DIM B7(20)
```

2. An array will be invalid if it is dimensioned in two DIM statements.

EXAMPLE 6-5: In the following program fragment, array A is invalid because it is dimensioned in two DIM statements, even though its subscript is the same in both statements.

```
10 DIM A(20), B(30)
20 DIM A(20), C(40)
```

6-3. Arrays and Loops

By combining arrays and loops you can create powerful BASIC programs that will perform many operations with relatively few lines. A simple program using loops and arrays can accomplish a great deal of processing. The FOR . . . NEXT loop is often used to manipulate arrays because the FOR . . . NEXT loop index provides a convenient subscript for "stepping through" all or part of an array.

A. Initializing an array

In BASIC, a common practice is to initialize an array to a predetermined value. Most BASIC interpreters set the value of variables to zero at the beginning of the program, but it is good programming practice to explicitly set to zero the variables used as accumulators. Also, variables that are used several times in a program must be set to zero each time before they are used.

In Example 6-2, an array of four elements was set to zero. Using similar techniques, you can set an array of any length to any desired number. By varying the parameters of the FOR . . . NEXT loop, parts of the array can be initialized to different values.

EXAMPLE 6-6: The following statements set N(1). . .N(500) to zero and N(501). . .N(1000) to 1.

```
10 DIM N(1000)
20 FOR I=1 TO 500
30    LET N(I)=0
40 NEXT I
50 FOR I=501 TO 1000
60    LET N(I)=1
70 NEXT I
```

EXAMPLE 6-7: The following statements set each element of the array S to the value of its own subscript.

```
10 DIM S(1000)
20 FOR I=1 TO 1000
30    S=I
40 NEXT I
```

The diagram below shows the values stored in a portion of the array S after execution of the program fragment.

S(498) S(499) S(500) S(501) S(502) S(503) S(504)

S . . .	498	499	500	501	502	503	504	. . .

B. Summing an array

It is often necessary to sum the values of all the individual elements in an array. This is easily accomplished by adding the values of the elements, one at a time, to a variable. This variable, sometimes called an *accumulator*, should be initialized to zero before the summing routine begins.

EXAMPLE 6-8: After values have been assigned to the array R in the following program, lines 100 to 120 sum all the values. A is set to zero in line 90, so that after each value of R is added to it in line 110, A will retain the sum.

```
10 DIM R(40)
   .
   .
   .
90 A=0
100 FOR I=1 TO 40
110    A=A+R(I)
120 NEXT I
```

When the loop terminates, A will contain the sum of all 40 values in array R. Note that the individual values in R are unchanged, so they remain available for further processing.

EXAMPLE 6-9: Often, the number of elements to be summed is not known until the program is run. In the following program, the number of values to be processed, N, is read in. Then the array V(1). . .V(N) is filled with data values. The N elements of the array are then summed, and the sum is printed.

```
10 DIM V(1000)
20 INPUT "Number of values"; N
30 FOR I=1 TO N
40    INPUT "Value"; V(I)
50 NEXT I
60 S=0
70 FOR I=1 TO N
80    LET S=S+V(I)
90 NEXT I
100 PRINT "The sum of the"; N; "values is"; S; "."
110 END
```

Display:

```
Number of values? 4
Value? 2
Value? 3
Value? 7
Value? 8
The sum of the 4 values is 20.
```

As an exercise, modify the program so that it uses only one FOR . . . NEXT loop and also checks the value of N to make certain that it is less than or equal to 1000.

C. Finding the largest or smallest value in an array

You can find the largest or smallest value in an array by placing an IF statement within the FOR . . . NEXT loop to test each array value as the loop is executed.

EXAMPLE 6-10: In the following program, the IF statement tests each value of array R to find the largest value. (Assume that R has already been initialized with positive values.)

```
100 L=0
110 FOR I=1 TO 40
120    IF R(I)>L THEN L=R(I)
130 NEXT I
```

As the loop is executed, the IF statement compares each of the 40 values of R with L. If R(I) is larger than L, then L is set to the new, larger value. Otherwise, no action is taken and the loop continues. After the loop terminates, L contains the greatest value of all the elements of R. The elements of R, however, remain unchanged. A similar loop may be used to find the smallest value in an array.

```
200 S=999999
210 FOR I=1 TO 40
220    IF R(I)<S THEN S=R(I)
230 NEXT I
```

D. Searching for a target value

The FOR . . . NEXT loop may be used to search for a specific value in an array and report its position, if found. The search is accomplished by initializing a variable to the target value and then using an IF statement to compare this value to each of the array elements. If one of the array elements matches the target value, the IF statement exits the loop and the loop index marks the target value's position. Remember that the value of the loop index is preserved when the IF statement causes an early exit from the loop.

EXAMPLE 6-11: The following program searches the values of S to find the target value T.

```
10 DIM S(5)
15 REM The values of S were defined earlier.
20 LET T=7
30 FOR I=1 TO 5
40    IF T=S(I) THEN 100
50 NEXT I
60 PRINT "The value"; T; "was not found in the array."
70 GOTO 200
100 PRINT "The value"; T; "was found in position"; I; "."
200 END
```

Display:

```
The value 7 was found in position 3.
```

	S(1)	S(2)	S(3)	S(4)	S(5)
S	2	8	7	8	3

6-4. Matrices

Thus far we have been visualizing the array variable as a row of numbered elements or boxes, where a particular element is accessed by a single subscript. This kind of array is sometimes called a *one-dimensional array*, or *vector*. BASIC also supports arrays with two subscripts, called *two-dimensional arrays*, or *matrices* (singular *matrix*). The two-dimensional matrix can be visualized as a wall of mailboxes in a post office.

EXAMPLE 6-12: Here is matrix M, dimensioned as DIM M(4,5), with five rows and six columns.

columns

		0	1	2	3	4	5
	0	3	6	6	8	2	9
	1	4	3	6	7	9	0
M rows	2	3	4	5	7	2	1
	3	2	1	0	3	4	0
	4	4	5	6	2	3	5

This matrix holds thirty values ($5 \times 6 = 30$), each of which can be accessed by specifying its row and column. For example, the value of M(0,5) is 9. The value of M(2,3) is 7. While the matrix is not actually stored in this tabular form within the computer memory, it is useful to visualize the matrix as presented here, with the first subscript corresponding to the row number and the second subscript corresponding to the column number.

A. The DIM statement is used to declare matrices.

Just as in one-dimensional arrays, the DIM statement is also used to declare matrices. The form is the same as for one-dimensional arrays, and arrays of both one and two dimensions may be intermixed in the same DIM statement. For example:

```
DIM M(4,5), I2(8,6), N(100)
DIM A(20), B(2,200), C(28)
```

EXAMPLE 6-13: A chessboard is an 8 × 8 matrix. You can describe the position of any piece with an ordered pair of integers. If your pieces are in rows 1 and 2, then your queen is in position, or element, (1,5) and your pawns are in (2,1), (2,2), (2,3), . . . , (2,8). In BASIC, a chessboard would be dimensioned C(8,8).

EXAMPLE 6-14: Seats in a classroom are another example of a matrix. Suppose there are seven rows with eight seats. This matrix would be dimensioned R(7,8), because the row number comes first. If there were eight rows of seven seats, the matrix would be dimensioned R(8,7).

As with one-dimensional arrays, the elements that have zeros as subscripts are often ignored. The chessboard matrix C(8,8) actually has nine rows and nine columns, but in this case it is easier to use only rows and columns numbered one through eight.

B. Matrices are often manipulated by nested FOR . . . NEXT loops.

Since each element in a matrix is described by a unique ordered pair of integers, it is easy to specify one element after another by using the indices of two FOR . . . NEXT loops. One row or column may be accessed by using a constant for the row or column subscript and a loop index for the other subscript.

1. You can use a nested FOR . . . NEXT loop to set a matrix to zero.

EXAMPLE 6-15: The following program sets a 2 × 3 matrix to zero, one element at a time. The values of the subscripts are printed for each iteration of the loops, so you can see how the row and column are generated for each element in the matrix.

```
1Ø DIM T(2,3)
2Ø PRINT " Subscripts for"
21 PRINT "  cells which"
22 PRINT "have been zeroed."
3Ø FOR R=1 TO 2
4Ø    FOR C=1 TO 3
5Ø        PRINT R, C
6Ø        LET T(R,C)=Ø
7Ø    NEXT C
8Ø NEXT R
9Ø END
```

Output:

```
    Subscripts for
      cells which
  have been zeroed.
  1              1
  1              2
  1              3
  2              1
  2              2
  2              3
```

		columns		
		1	**2**	**3**
T	**1**	(1,1) Ø	(1,2) Ø	(1,3) Ø
rows	**2**	(2,1) Ø	(2,2) Ø	(2,3) Ø

2. You can use a nested FOR . . . NEXT loop to sum the values held in the elements of the matrix.

EXAMPLE 6-16: The following program fragment sums the contents of a 1000 × 2000 array.

```
1Ø DIM B(1ØØØ,2ØØØ)
2Ø LET S=Ø
3Ø FOR I=1 TO 1ØØØ
4Ø    FOR J=1 TO 2ØØØ
5Ø        LET S=S+B(I,J)
6Ø    NEXT J
7Ø NEXT I
8Ø PRINT "The sum is"; S; "."
9Ø END
```

Obviously, this array is too large to be shown in the mailbox form we used earlier, and few computers could even hold the entire array in memory at one time. Yet the routine for summing the array takes only a few statements. Line 50 would be executed two million times!

3. You can access any particular element in a matrix by specifying its subscripts, either as constants, such as B(593,1482); as variables, such as B(I,J); or as expressions, such as B(I+1,J−1).

EXAMPLE 6-17: In an example used earlier, a classroom had seven rows of seats, and each row had eight seats. Let's say that you want to know the name of the student who sits in the third seat of the fourth row. The subscripts for this seat would be (4,3). Using the array R, the location of the seat would be R(4,3). The following program accepts a row and seat number as input, and outputs the name of the student assigned to this seat. (We are assuming that the names of the students have been assigned previously to their seat locations.)

```
10 DIM R$(7,8)
  .
  .
  .
100 INPUT "Enter row number and seat number"; R1, S1
110 PRINT
120 PRINT "The name of the student in row"; R1; ", seat"; S1
130 PRINT "is "; R$(R1, S1)
```

Display:

```
Enter row number and seat number? 4, 3

The name of the student in row 4 , seat 3
is James Capper
```

C. A matrix may have more than two dimensions.

Some versions of BASIC have restrictions on the number of dimensions they permit. However, you are unlikely to need more than three dimensions. Figure 6-1 illustrates a three-dimensional array.

1. Higher-dimensional arrays are declared in the same way as one- and two-dimensional arrays. Here is a DIM statement with arrays of one, two, three, and seven dimensions:

```
DIM A(70), B(3,5), D(4,10,20), F(2,4,3,5,4,6,7)
```

2. Higher-dimensional arrays may consume huge amounts of storage, since the total number of elements is the product of all the dimensions. For example, the seven-dimensional array F, above, contains 20,160 elements.
3. Higher-dimensional arrays are accessed in ways similar to one- and two-dimensional arrays.

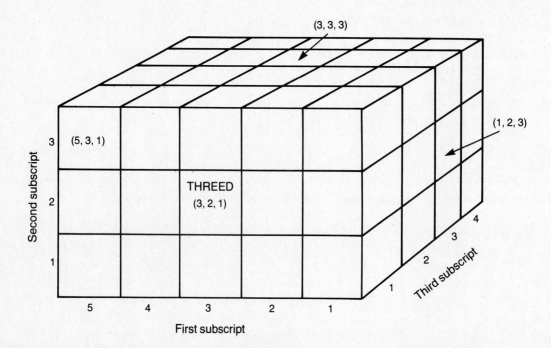

Figure 6-1

EXAMPLE 6-18: The following program uses FOR . . . NEXT loops to set the three-dimensional array D(4,10,20) to zero.

```
10 DIM D(4,10,20)
20 FOR I=0 TO 4
30    FOR J=0 TO 10
40       FOR K=0 TO 20
50          LET D(I,J,K)=0
60       NEXT K
70    NEXT J
80 NEXT I
90 END
```

EXAMPLE 6-19: Holding one subscript constant in a higher-dimensional array allows us to operate on one level of the array. In the following program, the constant 2 is used in the three dimensional array D so that the program will access the values of the array at that level only.

```
10 DIM D(4,10,20)
20 FOR J=0 TO 10
30    FOR K=0 TO 20
40       D(2,J,K)=2
50    NEXT K
60 NEXT J
70 END
```

6-5. READ, DATA, and RESTORE

In your BASIC programs you will often need to initialize variables, particularly arrays, to preset values. While you could accomplish this by a series of assignment statements, an easier way is to use READ and DATA statements.

The READ statement contains a list of variables, and the DATA statement contains a list of data items. When the READ statement is executed, it assigns the values in the DATA statement to the corresponding variables in the READ statement. This READ–DATA pair is convenient for initializing variables and arrays and is often used to simplify program testing.

A. The form of the READ statement

The READ statement has the form

> READ *variable 1, variable 2, . . .*

where the variable in the list may be either numeric or string. There is no limit to the number of variables that can be listed in a READ statement other than the limit on the line length imposed by your version of BASIC. Here are two examples of READ statements:

```
READ A, B(I)
READ C, D, A$, B2$
```

B. The form of the DATA statement

The DATA statement has the form

> DATA *data item 1, data item 2, . . .*

where the data items may be either numeric or string data. The data items are separated by commas. For example:

```
DATA 3, 5, 7, 2.3, -71, 24.3E03
DATA 5.6, 7, NEW JERSEY, NEW YORK
```

1. The numeric data in DATA statements must consist of legal BASIC numeric constants. There can be no commas in the constant, because BASIC assumes that a comma marks the end of the data item. Plus or minus signs may be used; if there is no sign, the value is assumed to be positive. Decimal points are permitted; if there is no decimal point, one is assumed to follow the last digit in the number. Exponential format is also permitted.
2. The string data in DATA statements consist of legal BASIC string constants. Leading blanks are ignored. If a comma is part of the string, then the whole string must be enclosed in quotation marks; otherwise the comma is assumed to mark the end of the string data item. To include a quotation mark as part of a quoted string, two quotation marks must be entered.
3. All the DATA lines in a BASIC program make up a single list, no matter how many or how few items there are in each line, and no matter where the lines are located in the program.

C. The variables in READ statements must correspond to the data items in DATA statements.

Whenever a READ statement is executed, the items in the DATA list are assigned to the corresponding variables in the READ statement. Therefore, it's important to make certain that you are assigning string data to string variables and numeric data to numeric variables. You must also be careful to make sure that data items are assigned to the desired variables. The following program shows a simple READ–DATA combination:

```
10 READ A, B, C$
20 DATA 2, 3, HELLO
30 PRINT A; B, C$
100 END
```

Display:

```
2 3          HELLO
```

D. BASIC uses a "pointer" as a place keeper for items in DATA lines.

The pointer in a DATA statement indicates the items to be accessed. When execution begins, this pointer is set to the first data item in the first DATA statement in the program. Each time a value is assigned to a variable in a READ statement, the pointer is advanced to the next data item. (Remember that all the DATA statements in the program are aggregated into a single list.)

EXAMPLE 6-20: In the following program, the DATA lines appear both before and after the READ statement (not good programming style), and the READ statement obtains its data items from both line 10 (B1, B2, B3, B1$) and line 30 (B2$).

```
10 DATA 2, 5, 6, BASIC
20 READ B1, B2, B3, B1$, B2$
30 DATA PROGRAMMING PRACTICE
40 PRINT B1, B2, B3
60 PRINT B1$; " "; B2$
100 END
```

Display:

```
2         5         6
BASIC PROGRAMMING PRACTICE
```

If there are more data items in DATA statements than corresponding variables in READ statements, the excess data items are simply ignored. If there are too few data items, execution will terminate, usually with an error message like OUT OF DATA.

E. The RESTORE statement starts the DATA list over again.

The form of the RESTORE statement is

$$\boxed{\text{RESTORE}}$$

Whenever a RESTORE statement is executed, BASIC moves the READ–DATA pointer back to the first item in the first DATA line in the program (that is, to the beginning of the data list). In most versions of BASIC, the pointer cannot be moved to any other position in the list.

EXAMPLE 6-21: The following program uses a RESTORE statement so that the DATA statement can be read twice.

```
10 READ A, S$, N$
20 RESTORE
30 READ A1, S1$, N1$
100 DATA 32, M, JOSEPH
200 PRINT A, S$, N$
210 PRINT A1, S1$, N1$
500 END
```

Display:

```
32          M          JOSEPH
32          M          JOSEPH
```

F. A common use of READ–DATA is to initialize arrays or matrices.

In the following program, S$(I) contains a salesperson's name and A(I) contains the amount the salesperson sold during the current month. Each time the FOR . . . NEXT loop is executed, the READ statement accesses the corresponding values in the DATA statements.

```
10 REM N IS THE NUMBER OF SALESPERSONS
20 N=5
30 FOR I=1 TO N
40 READ S$(I), A(I)
50 NEXT I
60 DATA JONES, 273.50, SMITH, 492.30, DOE, 19.47
70 DATA BARNEY, 1024.93, ARNIE, 23.20
```

RAISE YOUR GRADES

Can you explain. . . ?

☑ the permissible subscript forms for BASIC arrays
☑ the purpose of declaring arrays
☑ when it is necessary to use a DIM statement
☑ how one-dimensional arrays are declared and stored
☑ how a FOR . . . NEXT loop can be used to set an array to zero
☑ how a FOR . . . NEXT loop can be used to sum the elements of an array
☑ how two-dimensional arrays are declared and stored
☑ how nested FOR . . . NEXT loops can be used to set a matrix to zero
☑ how nested FOR . . . NEXT loops can be used to sum the elements of a matrix
☑ how the READ–DATA combination functions
☑ the purpose of the RESTORE statement

SUMMARY

1. A scalar variable is a simple variable that holds one value.
2. An array variable is a collection of values. Each value, or element, functions individually like a simple variable. Array variables are named in the same way as simple variables.
3. The elements in an array are numbered starting with zero, and the number is called a subscript. For example, $X(0)$ is the first element of X, $A(2)$ is the third element of A, and $H(10)$ is the eleventh element of H.
4. Any numeric constant, variable, or expression may be used as a subscript. A subscripted variable may be used as a subscript of another variable.
5. A one-dimensional array may be visualized as a row of boxes. The entire row is the array variable, and a subscript identifies each box (element).
6. BASIC also supports two-dimensional arrays, or matrices. Two subscripts identify each element of the two-dimensional array, one for the row and one for the column.
7. Many implementations of BASIC allow arrays with three or more dimensions. A subscript identifies each dimension.
8. An array is declared in a DIM statement, which must appear in the program before the array is used. The DIM statement reserves memory space for all the elements of the declared arrays. Arrays of any number of dimensions may be declared in the same DIM statement.
9. BASIC automatically dimensions array elements that contain eleven or fewer elements. Arrays that contain more than eleven elements must be dimensioned in a DIM statement.
10. The FOR . . . NEXT loop may be used to generate a series of values for the subscript of an array, thus making it possible to process an entire array one element at a time. Nested loops are often used to manipulate an array of more than one dimension.
11. The READ statement assigns the values in the DATA statement to the corresponding variables in the READ statement.
12. The variables in the READ statement must correspond to the values in the DATA statement or statements.
13. The "pointer" in the DATA statement indicates the data item to be accessed.
14. In most versions of BASIC, the RESTORE statement returns the pointer to the beginning of the DATA list.

RAPID REVIEW   Answers

True or False?

1. An element of an array variable is like a simple (scalar) variable.   True
2. To set an array of 500 elements to zero, 500 LET statements are required.   False
3. Several different array variables may be declared in one DIM statement.   True
4. More than one DIM statement may be used in a program.   True
5. In most versions of BASIC, RESTORE starts the DATA list from the beginning again.   True
6. In BASIC, the subscript may be any expression that yields a numeric quantity within the declared range.   True
7. A DATA statement must appear before a READ statement.   False
8. An array can be dimensioned more than once in a program.   False
9. $(3 * I - 2)$ is a valid subscript.   True

Fill in the blanks

1. Each element in an array is identified by its _____ .   subscript
2. No DIM statement is needed to declare an array of _____ or fewer elements.   eleven
3. A two-dimensional array is called a _____ .   matrix

Multiple choice

1. Which of the following specifications can be used to declare an array capable of storing 18 values?

   (*a*) A(12)   (*c*) C(1,2,2)
   (*b*) B(3,2)   (*d*) D(2,2)   *c*

2. DIM L(3,15), T(20) has already appeared in a program. Which of the following statements can follow it?

   (*a*) DIM B(7), L(3,15)
   (*b*) DIM L(15), A(5)
   (*c*) DIM C(3Ø), T(2Ø)
   (*d*) DIM A(3,15), B(2Ø)   *d*

3. The last element in the array T(3,5) is

   (*a*) T(3,3)   (*c*) T(3,5)
   (*b*) T(5,3)   (*d*) T(5,5)   *c*

SOLVED PROBLEMS

PROBLEM 6-1 Write a DIM statement for a vector of 100 string elements.

Answer:

```
DIM I$(99)
```

Vector arrays have only one subscript; this vector can be visualized as a row of 100 boxes.

PROBLEM 6-2 Write a DIM statement for a two-dimensional matrix of 25 elements.

Answer:

```
DIM T(4,4)
```

Two-dimensional arrays have two subscripts and can be visualized as mailboxes arranged in rows and columns. 5 × 5 is the only arrangement that will provide 25 elements.

PROBLEM 6-3 Write a DIM statement for a matrix that will hold values for the monthly rainfall for the 50 states.

Answer:

```
DIM S2(49,11)
```

Conceptually, this array is a table of 50 rows, one for each state, and 12 columns, one for each month. The name of the state is not stored in the matrix; the programmer must associate a row subscript with each state. For example, the state names might be alphabetized and the numbers 1 to 50 assigned to them in order: state 1 is Alabama, state 20 is Maryland, and state 50 is Wyoming.

PROBLEM 6-4 Write a DIM statement for a string vector that will hold the names of the 50 states.

Answer:

```
DIM A$(49)
```

This is the array needed to hold the state names for Problem 6-3.

PROBLEM 6-5 Write a short program that will print "I will write powerful programs" 100 times.

Answer:

```
20 FOR I=1 TO 100
30    PRINT "I will write powerful programs."
40 NEXT I
50 END
```

PROBLEM 6-6 Write a program that uses five nested FOR ... NEXT loops to set all the elements of the five-dimensional matrix I(3,5,2,4,2) to 1.

Answer:

```
20 DIM I(3,5,2,4,2)
110 FOR I1=0 TO 3
120    FOR I2=0 TO 5
130       FOR I3=0 TO 2
140          FOR I4=0 TO 4
150             FOR I5=0 TO 2
160                I(I1,I2,I3,I4,I5)=1
200             NEXT I5
210          NEXT I4
220       NEXT I3
230    NEXT I2
140 NEXT I1
300 END
```

Comment: A FOR ... NEXT loop is needed for each of the subscripts in order to uniquely specify each of the 1,080 elements in matrix I.

PROBLEM 6-7 Write a program that will generate and print the following numbers in the arrangement shown.

```
11  12  13  14  15
21  22  23  24  25
31  32  33  34  35
41  42  43  44  45
51  52  53  54  55
```

Answer:

```
20 DIM M(5, 5)
30 FOR I=1 TO 5
40    FOR J=1 TO 5
50       M(I, J)=I*10+J
60    NEXT J
70 NEXT I
100 FOR I=1 TO 5
110    FOR J=1 TO 5
120       PRINT M(I,J);
130    NEXT J
140    PRINT
150 NEXT I
200 END
```

Comment: The first digit in each number is produced by the loop that generates the values of I. The second digit in each number is produced by the loop that generates the values of J.

PROBLEM 6-8 When the matrix X(5,5) is printed, the 1's form an X:

```
1   Ø   Ø   Ø   1
Ø   1   Ø   1   Ø
Ø   Ø   1   Ø   Ø
Ø   1   Ø   1   Ø
1   Ø   Ø   Ø   1
```

Write a program that generates the values of matrix X and then prints them in the form shown above.

Answer:

```
20 DIM X(5, 5)
30 FOR I=1 TO 5
40    FOR J=1 TO 5
50        X(I, J)=Ø
60    NEXT J
70 NEXT I
100 FOR I=1 TO 5
110    X(I, I)=1
120    X(6-I, I)=1
130 NEXT I
200 FOR I=1 TO 5
210    FOR J=1 TO 5
220        PRINT X(I, J);
230    NEXT J
240    PRINT
250 NEXT I
300 END
```

Comment: Lines 30 through 70 place zeros in all the elements of X that will be used to print zeros. (The elements with zeros as subscripts will not be used.) Lines 100 through 130 set to 1 the values that will be used to form the X. (Notice that the index I is used twice.) Lines 200 through 250 print the matrix; they correspond to lines 30–70 in structure. 240 PRINT is used to end each printed line; otherwise, the semicolon at the end of 220 would cause all the values to be printed on one line.

PROBLEM 6-9 Write a program that will print the same results as in Problem 6-8, but will eliminate the spaces between the numbers. The output should look like this:

```
10001
Ø1Ø1Ø
ØØ1ØØ
Ø1Ø1Ø
1ØØØ1
```

Answer: Use a two-dimensional string array (X$) in the same program structure as in Problem 6-8.

```
20 DIM X$(5, 5)
30 FOR I=1 TO 5
40    FOR J=1 TO 5
50        X$(I, J)="Ø"
60    NEXT J
70 NEXT I
```

(*continued*)

(*continued*)

```
100 FOR I=1 TO 5
110    X$(I, I)="1"
120    X$(6-I, I)="1"
130 NEXT I
200 FOR I=1 TO 5
210    FOR J=1 TO 5
220       PRINT X$(I, J);
230    NEXT J
240    PRINT
250 NEXT I
300 END
```

PROBLEM 6-10 Write a program that declares a two-dimensional matrix to hold a student ID number, six test grades, and the test average for each of 25 students. Have the program read the I.D. and grades and then print the I.D. and test grade average for each student. The average should be rounded to an integer after it is calculated.

Answer:

```
20 DIM S(25, 7)
30 PRINT "Enter the student ID number, and then the six grades,"
31 PRINT "one after each prompt. (ID of zero terminates.)"
40 FOR I=1 TO 25
50    INPUT "ID number"; S(I, 0)
55    IF S(I, 0)=0 THEN 115
60    FOR G=1 TO 6
70       PRINT "Enter test grade"; G;
80       INPUT S(I, G)
90    NEXT G
100 NEXT I
110 PRINT "The grades for 25 students have been entered."
111 PRINT
114 REM Adjust loop index to reflect actual number of students.
115 N=I-1
195 REM Sum each student's grades, calculate and store average.
200 FOR I=1 TO N
210    T=0
220    FOR J=1 TO 6
230       T=T+S(I,J)
240    NEXT J
250    S(I, 7)=T/6
260 NEXT I
295 PRINT
296 PRINT "Student number    Average grade"
297 PRINT "--------------    -------------"
300 FOR I=1 TO N
310    PRINT "   "; S(I, 0), "      "; S(I, 7)
320 NEXT I
330 END
```

PROBLEM 6-11 Which of the following array elements have invalid BASIC subscripts?

(*a*) B(3)　　　　(*d*) B(K+1)
(*b*) B(K)　　　　(*e*) B(-3)
(*c*) B(D$)　　　　(*f*) B(1.1)

Answer:　The subscripts in (*c*) and (*e*) are invalid. The subscript must have a numerical value, so a string can't be a subscript, as in (*c*). The subscript cannot be negative, as in (*e*).

PROBLEM 6-12 Which of the following program fragments are correct?

(*a*)
```
10 FOR I=1 TO 10
20    A(I)=0
30 NEXT I
40 A(0)=20
```

(*b*)
```
10 B(7)=0
20 DIM B(8)
```

(*c*)
```
10 FOR M=0 TO 10
20    FOR N=0 TO 10
30       P(M, N)=1
40    NEXT N
50 NEXT M
```

(*d*)
```
1 FOR P=0 TO 20
2    P1(P)=P
3 NEXT P
```

(*e*)
```
10 FOR I=1 TO 10
20    FOR J=0 TO 10
30       FOR K=0 TO 10
40          T(I,J,K)=1
50       NEXT K
60    NEXT J
70 NEXT I
1000 END
```

Answer: The programs in (*a*), (*c*), and (*e*) are correct. When an array first appears in a program, BASIC automatically allocates space for eleven elements in each dimension, numbered 0 through 10. Since these dimensions have already been set, line 20 in (*b*) is an attempt to redimension array B, which is not allowed. In (*d*), array P1 will exceed eleven elements, so a DIM statement is needed.

PROBLEM 6-13 Which of the following DIM statements (or combinations of statements) are valid?

(*a*) `10 DIM A(5), B(6,10)`

(*b*) `10 DIMENSION B2(10), A2(20)`

(*c*)
```
10 DIM A1(20), B1(20)
20 DIM X(100), C2(100)
```

(*d*)
```
10 DIM K(100), M(100)
20 DIM K(100), M(80)
```

(*e*) `10 DIM P(20) Q(20)`

Answer: (*a*) and (*c*) are valid. In (*b*), the word DIMENSION is incorrect; it should be DIM. In (*d*), the arrays are dimensioned twice, even though the dimension of array K doesn't change. In (*e*), the comma is missing after P(20).

PROBLEM 6-14 How many elements are in each of the following arrays?

(*a*) D(8, 3)   (*d*) G(4, 6, 8)
(*b*) E(5)   (*e*) H(11)
(*c*) F(101, 2)

Answer: (*a*) 36, (*b*) 6, (*c*) 306, (*d*) 315, (*e*) 12. Remember that each dimension begins with subscript 0.

PROBLEM 6-15 Write a program fragment that reads the average temperature each day for a month, stores each temperature in an array, and stores the number of days at each temperature in another array. Assume that temperatures vary between 1 and 100 degrees, inclusive.

Answer:

```
20 DIM T(30), D(100)
30 PRINT "As the number of each day is printed,"
40 PRINT "enter the average temperature for that day."
50 FOR I=1 TO 30
60     PRINT "Day"; I;
70     INPUT T(I)
80 NEXT I
90 FOR J=1 TO 100
100    D(J)=0
110 NEXT J
120 FOR K=1 TO 30
130    D(T(K))=D(T(K))+1
140 NEXT K
150 FOR I=1 TO 100
160    PRINT "Days with temp"; I; ":";
165    REM Skip bar if there are no days with this temperature.
170    IF D(I)=0 THEN 200
175    FOR J=1 TO D(I)
180       PRINT "*";
190    NEXT J
200    PRINT
210 NEXT I
```

Comment: This program stores values for a 30-day period. The length of the period could be changed by altering the DIM statement and lines 50 and 120. Lines 90–110 set the array D to zero, because the elements of D will be used to add up the number of days with temperatures equal to the subscript. That is, two days with temperatures of 75 will make D(75) equal to 2. Notice that in line 130, the value of T(K) (the temperature for day K) becomes the subscript for D. Lines 150–210 print a bar graph, using one asterisk for each day at a given temperature. The loop in lines 175–190 uses the number of days D(I) as the end value of the FOR . . . NEXT loop. Part of this bar graph would look like this:

```
Day with temp 1 :*
  .
  .
  .
Day with temp 99 :****
Day with temp 100 :**
```

PROBLEM 6-16 Write a program that sets the value of each element in a three-dimensional array to the value of the second subscript.

Answer:

```
10 REM This program sets each element in S equal to
11 REM the second subscript of the element.
20 DIM S(3, 7, 6)
30 FOR I=0 TO 3
40     FOR J=0 TO 7
50         FOR K=0 TO 6
60             S(I, J, K)=J
70         NEXT K
80     NEXT J
90 NEXT I
200 END
```

PROBLEM 6-17 Write a program fragment that sets all odd-numbered elements of K2(100) to 1, and all even-numbered elements to 2.

Answer:

```
20 DIM K2(100)
30 FOR I=1 TO 100 STEP 2
40    K2(I)=1
50    K2(I+1)=2
60 NEXT I
70 FOR I1=1 TO 100
80    PRINT K2(I1),
90 NEXT I1
100 END
```

Comment: Line 30 selects all the odd numbers, starting with 1 and ending with 99, so that the maximum subscript in line 50 will be 100. The comma in line 80 causes the values of K2 to be printed across the screen. Depending on your terminal, the display will look something like this:

```
1         2         1         2         1         2
1         2         1         2         1         2
 . . .
```

PROBLEM 6-18 Write a program fragment that generates the first 20 Fibonacci numbers, stores them in an array, and then prints the contents of the array, one number to a line. The Fibonacci series is 1, 1, 2, 3, 5, . . . , where each number is the sum of the preceding two numbers.

Answer:

```
20 DIM F(20)
30 F(1)=1
40 F(2)=1
50 FOR I=3 TO 20
60    F(I)=F(I-1)+F(I-2)
70 NEXT I
80 FOR J=1 TO 20
90    PRINT F(J)
100 NEXT J
110 END
```

PROBLEM 6-19 Write a program that reads daily sales figures from four stores for a month and then generates total daily sales for all stores, total monthly sales for each store, and total monthly sales for all stores.

Answer:

```
20 DIM S(31, 4), T1(31), T2(4)
25 REM Zero the accumulators
30 T=0
40 FOR I=1 TO 31
50    T1(I)=0
60 NEXT I
70 FOR I=1 TO 4
80    T2(I)=0
90 NEXT I
100 REM Fill the sales array with sales figures for the month
```
(continued)

(continued)

```
110 INPUT "Enter the number of days in this month"; D
120 PRINT "Enter sales for stores 1 - 4, separated by commas,"
130 PRINT "after each day."
140 PRINT
150 PRINT " Day    Sales (Stores 1, 2, 3, 4)"
160 PRINT
170 FOR I=1 TO D
180   PRINT I;
190   INPUT S(I, 1), S(I, 2), S(I, 3), S(I, 4)
200 NEXT I
210 REM Total the sales for each day in T1
220 FOR I=1 TO D
230    FOR J=1 TO 4
240    T1(I)=T1(I)+S(I, J)
250       T2(J)=T2(J)+S(I, J)
260       T=T+S(I, J)
270    NEXT J
280 NEXT I
290 REM Print the results
300 PRINT
310 PRINT C$
320 PRINT "     Total sales by store for the month"
330 PRINT "     ---------------------------------"
340 PRINT "Store 1      Store 2      Store 3      Store 4"
350 PRINT
360 PRINT "$"; T2(1), "$"; T2(2), "$"; T2(3), "$"; T2(4)
370 PRINT
380 INPUT "Press return to continue"; A$
390 PRINT "Total sales for each day"
400 PRINT "------------------------"
410 C1=INT((D+1)/2)
420 FOR I=1 TO (D+1)/2
430    PRINT I; "   $"; T1(I),
440    IF I+C1>D THEN 460
450    PRINT I+C1; "   $"; T1(I+C1)
460 NEXT I
470 PRINT
480 PRINT
490 INPUT "Press return to continue"; A$
500 PRINT "Total sales for all stores for the month"
510 PRINT "----------------------------------------"
520 PRINT "               $"; T
530 END
```

PROBLEM 6-20 Use FOR ... NEXT loops and PRINT statements to output data from the shaded areas of array I1 below.

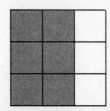

Answer:

```
100 FOR I=1 TO 3
110    FOR J=1 TO 2
120       PRINT I1(I, J);
130    NEXT J
140    PRINT
150 NEXT I
```

PROBLEM 6-21 Use FOR . . . NEXT loops and PRINT statements to output data from the shaded areas of array I2 below.

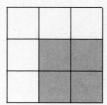

Answer:

```
100 FOR I=2 TO 3
110    FOR J=2 TO 3
120       PRINT I2(I, J);
130    NEXT J
140    PRINT
150 NEXT
```

PROBLEM 6-22 Use FOR . . . NEXT loops and PRINT statements to output data from the shaded areas of array I3 below.

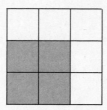

Answer:

```
100 FOR I=2 TO 3
110    FOR J=1 TO 2
120       PRINT I3(I, J);
130    NEXT J
140    PRINT
150 NEXT I
```

PROBLEM 6-23 Use FOR . . . NEXT loops and PRINT statements to output data from the shaded areas of array I4 below.

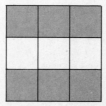

Answer:

```
100 FOR J=1 TO 3
110    PRINT I4(1, J);
120 NEXT J
130 PRINT
140 PRINT
150 FOR J=1 TO 3
160    PRINT I4(3, J);
170 NEXT J
180 PRINT
```

Comment: A simpler way to write this program is to use three PRINT statements:

```
100 PRINT I4(1,1); I4(1,2); I4(1,3)
110 PRINT
120 PRINT I4(3,1); I4(3,2); I4(3,3)
```

PROBLEM 6-24 One day last year it rained 7.3 inches. Write a program fragment that will locate and report which day this was, assuming the precipitation records are stored in the array R(1), . . . , R(365).

Answer:

```
20 DIM R(365)
30 REM For the purposes of this exercise, assume that
40 REM the array R has been initialized with precipitation amounts.
50 T=7.3
60 FOR I=1 TO 365
70    IF R(I)=T THEN 120
80 NEXT I
90 PRINT "Sorry, I can't find a day with precipitation"
100 PRINT "of"; T; "inches."
110 GOTO 140
120 PRINT "The precipitation amount"; T; "
130 PRINT "occurred on day"; I; "of the year."
140 END
```

PROBLEM 6-25 Write a program that reads data values and calculates five-part moving averages (the average of the data item and the two items before and two items after). Moving averages are used to smooth out variations in data series. Have the program print the original data and the smoothed data in a line graph.

Answer:

```
10 REM D is Data, S is Smoothed data, G$ is Graph, T is Total
20 DIM D(40), S(40), G$(10,40)
30 REM Initialize arrays.
40 REM Put a single blank in each element of G$
50 FOR I=1 TO 10
60    FOR J=1 TO 40
70       G$(I,J)=" "
80    NEXT J
90 NEXT I
95 REM Read values into D, and copy in S, so that first and last
96 REM two values of S will be filled.
```

(continued)

(continued)

```
100 FOR I=1 TO 40
110     READ D(I)
120     S(I)=D(I)
130 NEXT I
200 REM Calculate smoothed values for S: Find average of value of
210 REM D and two before and after, then enter in S
220 FOR I=3 TO 38
230     T=0
240     FOR J=I-2 TO I+2
250         T=T+D(J)
260         S(I)=T / 5
270     NEXT J
280 NEXT I
300 REM Create line graph, with values D and S as row subscripts
310 REM after normalizing them to values of 1 to 10
320 FOR I=1 TO 40
330     S1=(D(I)-40)/3
340     G$(S1, I)="-"
350     S2=(S(I)-40)/3
360     G$(S2,I)="*"
370 NEXT I
400 REM Print graph (upside down, with low numbers at bottom)
405 OPEN "O", 2, "SY1:B630OUT"
410 FOR I=10 TO 1 STEP -1
430     FOR J=1 TO 40
440 PRINT #2, G$(I,J);
450     NEXT J
470 NEXT I
480 CLOSE #2
1000 DATA 42,45.7,48.3,52.7,  49,50.3,54.7,  59,56.8,  60
1010 DATA 54,56.3,  58,  61,  59,  55,  61,65.9,  66,  66
1020 DATA 66,66.2,  68,  65,63.1,  60,  59,62.8,  64,  59
1030 DATA 58,  58,57.3,  49,  55,  56,  58,58.9,61.2,63.1
2000 END
```

Display:

```
                                  -
                         -******      -
             -  **        ***-              **
         -  -  -  **       --****-      -*
         *******  -                 ******
     - **     -
     **-                               -
    *
  *
```

Comment: The original data is plotted with a hyphen, and the smoothed series with an asterisk. When the two appear in the same position, the asterisk replaces the hyphen. Notice how the curve of asterisks changes less than the curve of hyphens.

PROBLEM 6-26 The following program is technically an infinite loop, but, in practice, it can only run until it uses up its data items. Provide enough data items in DATA statements so that the loop will run for three cycles.

```
10 READ A, B, C
20 PRINT A*B*C
```
(continued)

(continued)
```
3Ø  GOTO  1Ø
5Ø  DATA  1,  2,  3
1ØØ  END
```

Answer:

```
5Ø  DATA  1,  2,  3,  4,  5,  6
6Ø  DATA  7,  8,  9,  1Ø
```

Display:

```
6
12Ø
5Ø4
OUT  OF  DATA
```

Comment: To complete one cycle of the loop, the READ statement must access three values from the DATA statement. When the loop finishes its third cycle, only one value (10) is left in the second DATA statement. Therefore, when the program tries to complete a fourth repetition of the loop, not enough data will be available and the program will terminate with an error message.

PROBLEM 6-27 The following program will terminate with an error message. Find the error.

```
1Ø  READ  A,  B$
2Ø  READ  C,  D$
3Ø  READ  E,  F$
5Ø  READ  G,  H$
1ØØ  DATA  1,  2,  3,  ARE,  STRINGS,  8,  9,  CORRECT
1ØØØ  END
```

Answer: In line 30, BASIC will attempt to read the string STRINGS into the numeric variable E. This will cause a syntax error or an incorrect type error. Notice that BASIC will accept the character "2" as the value of B$ in line 10; however, characters can't be used as the value of a numeric variable. Since the program has already terminated, it won't run out of data in line 50.

7 ADVANCED CONTROL STRUCTURES

THIS CHAPTER IS ABOUT

- ☑ **Subprograms and Modular Design**
- ☑ **GOSUB and RETURN**
- ☑ **Menus**
- ☑ **ON . . . GOSUB**
- ☑ **ON . . . GOTO**
- ☑ **ON ERROR GOTO and RESUME**

7-1. Subprograms and Modular Design

In most computer languages a program can be constructed as a series of modules called *subroutines* or, more generally, *subprograms*. There are several advantages to modular program design. For example, several programmers can work on different parts of the same program at the same time. In some cases, a subprogram developed for one program can be used in another program, saving time in coding and testing. Also, if the same procedure is repeated more than once in the program, it need only be coded once as a subprogram and then used repeatedly.

BASIC subroutines are not as powerful as subroutines in many of the other programming languages. Still, if constructed properly, BASIC subroutines can be extremely effective and useful. For example, by using BASIC subroutines, you can

- organize a program into units, which simplifies coding, testing, and program design
- code a block of statements that can then be used at other points in the program
- simplify the branching structure of a program, which makes the program easier to follow

7-2. GOSUB and RETURN

In BASIC, a subroutine is simply a group of lines that are branched to and executed and which then return control to the point in the program where the branch was initiated. The BASIC subroutine is implemented by two statements: GOSUB and RETURN. The GOSUB statement transfers control to the line in the program where you want to begin execution of the subroutine. The form of the GOSUB statement is

GOSUB *line number*

The GOSUB statement is similar to the GOTO statement in form and execution. The major difference is that BASIC records the line number of the GOSUB statement when it is executed. Also, the GOSUB statement is used in conjunction with a RETURN statement. When a RETURN statement is encountered, BASIC returns control to the statement following the GOSUB so that the program can continue execution. The form of the RETURN statement is

RETURN

The following diagrams illustrate the operation of a GOTO statement and the operation of the GOSUB–RETURN structure. In the first diagram, the GOTO statement at line 50 transfers control to line 600, skipping the lines from 60 to 600. Execution continues from line 600 to the END statement at line 630, where the program terminates. Line 60 will not be executed.

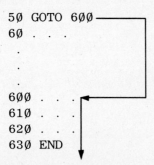

Replacing line 50 with a GOSUB statement and inserting a RETURN statement at line 625 creates a subroutine at lines 600–625. When the RETURN statement at line 625 is executed, it will cause a branch to line 60, the line following the GOSUB. Execution will then continue from line 60.

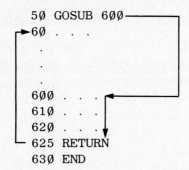

Many GOSUB statements may be used within a given program to execute a single subroutine, such as the one in lines 600–620. Since BASIC automatically records the number of the line following a GOSUB, executing a RETURN statement will always transfer control back to the appropriate line. Example 7-1 shows a subroutine that is referenced from two places.

EXAMPLE 7-1: The following program illustrates the value of using a subroutine to repeat an operation—in this case, printing a 5-line message. Look carefully at the output to see how control is transferred from one part of the program to another.

```
10 REM Program to show use of GOSUB and RETURN
20 GOSUB 100
30 PRINT "This line printed by main program"
40 GOSUB 100
50 PRINT "This line also printed by main program"
60 END
100 REM Beginning of BASIC subroutine
110 PRINT
120 PRINT "---------------------------------"
130 PRINT ": Printed by a BASIC subroutine :"
140 PRINT "---------------------------------"
150 PRINT
155 REM The next line is the end of the subroutine
160 RETURN
```

Display:

```
---------------------------------
: Printed by a BASIC subroutine :
---------------------------------

This line printed by main program

---------------------------------
: Printed by a BASIC subroutine :
---------------------------------

This line also printed by main program
```

The GOSUB statements at lines 20 and 40 transfer control to line 100. This subroutine, beginning at line 100, prints a message in a box, with a blank line above and below it. Then the RETURN statement at line 160 returns to the statement following each GOSUB.

You could create a subroutine similar to the GOSUB–RETURN structure by using two GOTO statements—one to transfer control to a block of statements, and another at the end of the block to transfer control back to the statement following the first GOTO. However, this will only work if you use the subroutine once and only if you access it from one GOTO statement. The reason is that the GOTO statement at the end of the subroutine can only transfer control back to one part of the program. The GOSUB–RETURN structure, on the other hand, always transfers control back to the statement following the last GOSUB executed, and thus can transfer control to various parts of the program.

7-3. Menus

A. Menus make programs easier to use.

More and more computer programs are written to be used by people who are not computer experts and who need a simple way of interacting with the program. Such programs must guide the user with information displayed on the screen. A common way of doing this is by using *menus*. A menu lists a number of program options from which the user may choose.

EXAMPLE 7-2: The following menu provides three options, each of which can be selected by entering the appropriate number.

```
Would you like to:

   1.   See instructions
   2.   Play the game
   3.   Quit

Enter the number of your choice.
```

Menus can be set up to provide dozens of options. In many cases, menus are nested in order to increase the number of options while retaining the menu's ease of use. Under this arrangement, a main menu offers a choice of submenus, and each submenu offers a list of options, including the choice of returning to the main menu. After the submenu action is performed, control returns to the submenu. The user can then choose another option from the submenu, or return to the main menu and from that level choose a different submenu.

B. Implementing menus in BASIC

Menu-driven BASIC programs are implemented as subroutines and are thus well-suited to modular program design. However, menus must be carefully structured in order to execute effectively. Figure 7-1 shows the program flow of a simple menu-driven program.

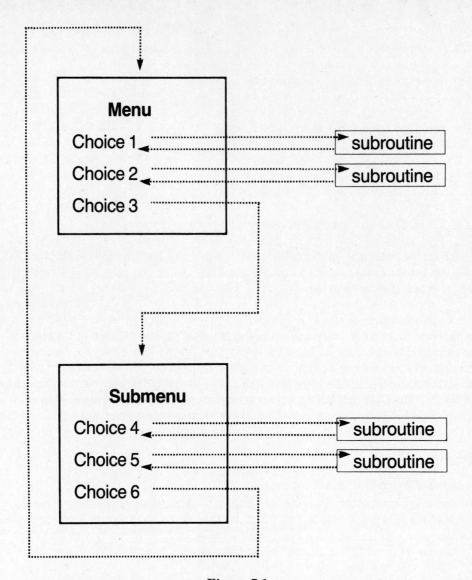

Figure 7-1

Choices 1 and 2 transfer control to subroutines, which return control to the main menu. Choice 3 transfers control to a submenu, which lists three additional choices. Choices 4 and 5 also transfer control to subroutines, but these subroutines return control to the submenu. Choice 6 transfers control back to the main menu.

The program structure of a simple BASIC menu generally consists of the following:

- a series of PRINT statements that display the user's options
- an INPUT statement or statements that are used to obtain the user's response
- a series of statements—often IF statements—that are used to evaluate the user's response and then branch to the appropriate subroutines

Two BASIC statements are especially well-suited to use in menus. These statements are ON . . . GOSUB, which is an extension of the standard GOSUB statement, and ON . . . GOTO, which is an extension of the standard GOTO statement.

7-4. ON . . . GOSUB

The ON . . . GOSUB statement transfers control to one of two or more designated subroutines according to the value of a variable or expression. The form of the ON . . . GOSUB statement is

ON *expression* GOSUB *line number, line number, . . .*

Each line number is the first line of a BASIC subroutine. When the ON . . . GOSUB statement is executed, control passes to one of the listed lines. The line chosen depends on the value of the expression. A value of 1 transfers control to the first line listed, a value of 2 transfers control to the first line listed, a value of 2 transfers control to the second line listed, and so forth. Once the line is selected, the transfer of control is the same as for a standard GOSUB.

The ON . . . GOSUB statement is particularly useful for returning control to a menu after an action is completed. As with the ordinary GOSUB statement, after the subroutine is completed, control returns to the statement following the ON . . . GOSUB, and this statement can then return control to the beginning of the menu procedure.

EXAMPLE 7-3: The following program, despite its length, is a rather simple example of a main menu and a submenu, implemented with ON . . . GOSUB and RETURN.

```
50 PRINT "Welcome to the Wonderful World of GOSUB"
60 PRINT
70 PRINT "          MAIN MENU''
80 PRINT
90 PRINT "   1   Friendly greetings"
100 PRINT "   2   A polite greeting"
110 PRINT "   3   A musical farewell"
120 PRINT
130 PRINT "Please type 1, 2, or 3, and press <RETURN>"
140 INPUT M
150 PRINT
160 ON M GOSUB 1000, 2000, 3000
170 PRINT
180 IF M<>3 THEN 60
190 GOTO 10000
1000      PRINT "          FRIENDLY GREETING MENU"
1010      PRINT
1020      PRINT "   1  Country greeting"
1030      PRINT "   2  City greeting"
1040      PRINT "   3  Singles-bar greeting"
1050      PRINT
1060      PRINT "Please type 1, 2, or 3, and press <RETURN>"
1070      INPUT M1
1080      PRINT
1090      ON M1 GOSUB 1500, 1600, 1700
1100      PRINT
1110      RETURN
1500        PRINT "Howdy, friend. Nice day, ain't it?"
1510        RETURN
1600          PRINT "Hey, watch it, bud."
1610          RETURN
1700            PRINT "I'm a Taurus. What's your sign?"
1710            RETURN
2000      PRINT "Good afternoon."
2010      RETURN
3000        PRINT "So long, it's been good to know you."
3010        RETURN
10000 END
```

When this program is run it will first display the main menu as follows:

```
Welcome to the Wonderful World of GOSUB

          MAIN MENU

     1    Friendly greetings
     2    A polite greeting
     3    A musical farewell

Please type 1, 2, or 3, and press <RETURN>
?
```

If you type the number 1 after the question mark, line 160 will access the submenu subroutine, which will produce the following display:

```
          FRIENDLY GREETING MENU

     1    Country greeting
     2    City greeting
     3    Singles-bar greeting

Please type 1, 2, or 3, and press <RETURN>
?
```

If you type the number 3 after the question mark, line 1090 will then GOSUB to line 1700, which will print

```
     I'm a Taurus. What's your sign?
```

Follow the program logic to determine what will happen when other options are selected.

7-5. ON . . . GOTO

The ON . . . GOTO statement transfers control to one of two or more designated lines according to the value of a variable or expression. As with the ordinary GOTO statement, program execution continues at the line that is branched to and does not return automatically to the starting point, as with the ON . . . GOSUB statement.

The ON . . . GOTO statement has the following form:

> ON *expression* GOTO *line number, line number, . . .*

If the value of the expression is 1, control passes to the first line number listed; if the value is 2, control passes to the second line number listed, and so forth.

The value of the expression must be between 1 and the maximum number of choices. If the value is less than 1 or too high, the ON . . . GOTO statement may not produce the desired results. Instead, you may get an error message or the transfer of control will fail to occur and the next sequential statement will be executed. Check your operator's manual to determine how your version of BASIC handles this problem. To ensure that an ON statement will execute properly, use an IF statement to test the value of the expression before the ON statement is executed and then make the necessary adjustments.

7-6. ON ERROR GOTO and RESUME

Various errors can occur while a program is running. These errors, called *execution time errors*, have many causes, the most common, perhaps, being improperly entered data. Generally, when

BASIC encounters this type of error, it will display an error message on the screen and terminate program execution. Some versions of BASIC, however, permit the program to intercept and handle errors. This is accomplished by the ON ERROR GOTO statement. When a BASIC program with an ON ERROR GOTO statement encounters an error, control transfers to the appropriate error-recovery routine. This procedure is called *error trapping* and allows the user to correct an error without having to restart the program.

When an ON ERROR GOTO statement is executed, it sets up the appropriate transfer of control but does not actually implement the transfer until an error occurs. When the system detects an error, the transfer (GOTO) is made, even if program execution has progressed far beyond the ON ERROR GOTO statement.

A. The form of the ON ERROR GOTO statement

The form of the ON ERROR GOTO statement will vary somewhat among the different versions of BASIC. The following are two forms that are in common use:

> ON ERROR GOTO *line number*

> ONERR GOTO *line number*

When an error occurs, control passes to the statement specified by the line number in the ON ERROR GOTO statement. However, ON ERROR GOTO will only "trap" errors that occur in subsequent statements in the program. Consequently, ON ERROR GOTO statements are usually placed at or near the beginning of a program.

B. ON ERROR GOTO may be used in conjunction with a RESUME statement.

The function of the RESUME statement varies depending on the form it takes. Three forms are in common use:

> RESUME

> RESUME NEXT

> RESUME *line number*

RESUME transfers control back to the statement in which the errors occurred. RESUME NEXT returns control to the statement following the statement in which the error was committed. RESUME *line number* transfers control to the specified line number.

C. ON ERROR GOTO does not distinguish among errors.

The ON ERROR GOTO statement only detects the occurrence of an error, it does not determine the specific type of error that has occurred. Most systems will set one variable to a code number indicating the specific error and another variable to the line in which the error occurred. By testing these variables the program can determine what error occurred and where. The program may then attempt to correct the error or may simply print a message and then terminate.

EXAMPLE 7-4: The following program asks the user to enter two numbers. The program then divides the first number by the second (line 40). If the divisor is zero, an error will occur; this error is handled by the ON ERROR GOTO statement.

```
10 ON ERROR GOTO 70
20 PRINT "PLEASE ENTER A AND B: ";
30 INPUT A,B
40 C=A/B
50 PRINT A; "DIVIDED BY "; B; " IS "; C
60 GOTO 20
70 PRINT "DIVIDE ERROR"
80 GOTO 20
90 END
```

RAISE YOUR GRADES

Can you explain . . . ?

☑ some advantages of using subroutines in computer programs
☑ how a simple BASIC subroutine is implemented
☑ the difference between the GOSUB statement and the GOTO statement
☑ the purpose of a menu
☑ the function of the ON . . . GOSUB statement
☑ how the ON . . . GOSUB statement differs from the ON . . . GOTO statement
☑ the purpose of the ON ERROR GOTO statement
☑ what "error trapping" means
☑ some forms of the RESUME statement

SUMMARY

1. A BASIC program may be written as a series of modules called subroutines or, more generally, subprograms. Among other benefits, subroutines facilitate testing and debugging.
2. BASIC subroutines are implemented by two statements: GOSUB and RETURN.
3. The GOSUB statement transfers control to the line in the program where execution of the subroutine is to begin.
4. The RETURN statement returns control to the statement following the GOSUB.
5. A menu provides a simple way of interacting with a program. A menu lists a number of program options and allows the user to select the desired choice.
6. The ON . . . GOSUB statement transfers control to one of two or more designated subroutines according to the value of a variable or expression. After the subroutine is completed, control returns to the statement following the ON . . . GOSUB.
7. The ON . . . GOTO statement transfers control to one of two or more designated lines according to the value of a variable or expression. Unlike the ON . . . GOSUB statement, control does not return to the starting point.
8. The ON ERROR GOTO statement permits the user to recover from errors during program execution by transferring control to the appropriate error recovery routine.
9. A RESUME statement is often used in conjunction with the ON ERROR GOTO statement. The function of the RESUME statement depends on the form it takes.

RAPID REVIEW   Answers

True or False?

1. A RETURN statement at the end of a subroutine automatically returns control to the line just before the last GOSUB statement.   False

2. The ON ERROR GOTO statement is often used with a RESUME statement.   True

3. BASIC permits only one GOSUB–RETURN pair in a program.   False

4. GOSUB 200 tells the computer to transfer control to line 200.   True

5. ON ERROR GOTO branches only if an error occurs.   True

Fill in the blanks

1. The last executed statement in a subroutine must be a _____
   statement.   RETURN

2. A _____ gives the user a list of options and specifies the key
   to be pressed to select the desired choice.   menu

3. If N = 2, the statement ON N GOSUB 400, 600 will transfer
   control to line _____.   600

4. IF X = 1, the statement ON X GOTO 200, 300, 400, 500 will
   transfer control to line _____.   200

Multiple choice

1. Given the program

```
100 GOSUB 500
110 STOP
500 PRINT "THIS IS ALL THAT THIS PROGRAM DOES"
510 RETURN
```

   which of the following will occur?

   (*a*) The program will terminate before it reaches line 500.
   (*b*) The program will not execute because a subroutine must be
   more than one line.
   (*c*) The program will execute and print the message in line 500.
   (*d*) The program will not execute because a program cannot begin
   with a GOSUB command.   *c*

2. What is incorrect in this program?

```
10 GOSUB 400
20 PRINT "WHAT NUMBER WOULD YOU LIKE SQUARED?"
30 INPUT N
40 LET X=N^2
60 GOTO 430
400 PRINT "THE SQUARE OF ";N; " IS "
410 PRINT X
420 RETURN
430 END
```

   (*a*) Line 10 directs control to the wrong line number.
   (*b*) The statement in line 10 should follow line 40 and precede line 60.
   (*c*) The statement in line 60 should follow line 420.
   (*d*) Line 400 is not a valid statement.   *b*

3. What is incorrect in this program?

```
10 REM "THIS PROGRAM AVERAGES TWO NUMBERS"
20 PRINT "TYPE IN TWO NUMBERS"
40 INPUT A, B
50 GOSUB 400
400 LET X=(A+B)/2
410 PRINT X
420 RETURN
```

(*a*) The subroutine creates an infinite loop.
(*b*) Line 420 should indicate what line to return to.
(*c*) The GOSUB statement should occur before line 40.
(*d*) Line 400 contains an incorrect statement.   *a*

SOLVED PROBLEMS

PROBLEM 7-1 Explain the structure of the simplest BASIC subroutine.

Answer: A simple BASIC subroutine is implemented by two statements: GOSUB and RETURN. The GOSUB statement transfers control to a line in the program where you want to begin execution of a subroutine. When the subroutine is completed, the RETURN statement returns control to the statement following the GOSUB.

PROBLEM 7-2 What is the output of this program?

```
10 GOSUB 400
20 GOSUB 400
30 GOSUB 400
40 END
400 PRINT "THIS IS A SUBROUTINE"
410 RETURN
```

Answer:

```
THIS IS A SUBROUTINE
THIS IS A SUBROUTINE
THIS IS A SUBROUTINE
```

PROBLEM 7-3 What is the output of this program?

```
10 GOSUB 600
20 PRINT "JUMPED OVER"
30 GOSUB 800
40 GOTO 900
600 PRINT "THE QUICK BROWN FOX"
610 RETURN
800 PRINT "THE LAZY DOG"
810 RETURN
900 END
```

Answer:

```
THE QUICK BROWN FOX
JUMPED OVER
THE LAZY DOG
```

PROBLEM 7-4 Why is it better to create subroutines by using the GOSUB–RETURN structure than by using GOTO statements?

Answer: While subroutines can be created with GOTO statements, these subroutines are extremely limited in operation. A subroutine created by GOTO statements can only be initiated from one GOTO statement, because the GOTO statement that terminates the subroutine can only transfer control to a single, designated point in the program. A subroutine created by GOSUB and RETURN statements, however, can be initiated from various GOSUB statements in different parts of the program, because the RETURN statement will always return control to the statement following the GOSUB that last transferred control to the subroutine.

PROBLEM 7-5 Explain the function of the ON . . . GOSUB statement.

Answer: The ON . . . GOSUB statement transfers control to one of two or more designated subroutines according to the value of a variable or expression. A value of 1 transfers control to the first line listed in the ON . . . GOSUB statement, a value of 2 transfers control to the second line listed, and so forth. As with the ordinary GOSUB, the ON . . . GOSUB statement is usually used in conjunction with a RETURN statement; after the subroutine is completed, control returns to the statement following the ON . . . GOSUB statement.

PROBLEM 7-6 What is the output of this program if the user enters the number 2?

```
10 PRINT "ENTER 1 OR 2"
20 INPUT X
30 ON X GOSUB 300, 400
40 GOTO 500
300 PRINT "YOU ENTERED NUMBER 1"
310 RETURN
400 PRINT "YOU ENTERED NUMBER 2"
410 RETURN
500 END
```

Answer:

```
YOU ENTERED NUMBER 2
```

PROBLEM 7-7 Using a nested FOR . . . NEXT loop, write a subroutine that will print 5 lines of 20 asterisks each, double spaced.

Answer:

```
10 GOSUB 700
15 PRINT
20 GOSUB 700
25 PRINT "NEXT LINE"
50 GOSUB 1700
60 GOSUB 1700
100 END
700 FOR N=1 TO 5
710 PRINT
720 FOR K=1 TO 20
730 PRINT "*";
740 NEXT K
750 NEXT N
760 RETURN
1700 FOR N=1 TO 5
1710 FOR K=1 TO 20
1720 PRINT "*";
1730 NEXT K
1740 PRINT
1750 NEXT N
1760 RETURN
```

PROBLEM 7-8 Write a program that asks for the number of children (up to 6) in the user's family, and then indicates whether the size of the family was average or larger or smaller than the average (2 or 3 children being the average).

Answer:

```
10 PRINT "ENTER THE NUMBER OF CHILDREN"
20 PRINT "DO NOT USE A NUMBER LARGER THAN 6"
30 INPUT N
40 ON N GOSUB 100, 200, 200, 300, 300, 300
50 GOTO 900
100 PRINT "YOUR FAMILY IS SMALLER THAN AVERAGE"
110 RETURN
200 PRINT "YOUR FAMILY IS AVERAGE IN SIZE"
210 RETURN
300 PRINT "YOUR FAMILY IS LARGER THAN AVERAGE"
310 RETURN
900 END
```

PROBLEM 7-9 Using ON . . . GOSUB, write a program that gives the user a choice of having the computer print either "hello" or "goodbye."

Answer:

```
10 PRINT "PRESS 1 TO PRINT HELLO"
20 PRINT "PRESS 2 TO PRINT GOODBYE"
30 INPUT N
40 ON N GOSUB 100, 200
50 GOTO 300
100 PRINT "HELLO'
110 RETURN
200 PRINT "GOODBYE"
210 RETURN
300 END
```

PROBLEM 7-10 Rewrite the program in Problem 7-9 using ON . . . GOTO.

Answer:

```
10 PRINT "PRESS 1 TO PRINT HELLO"
20 PRINT "PRESS 2 TO PRINT GOODBYE"
30 INPUT N
40 ON N GOTO 100, 200
50 GOTO 300
100 PRINT "HELLO"
110 GO TO 300
200 PRINT "GOODBYE"
210 GOTO 300
300 END
```

PROBLEM 7-11 Explain the function of the ON ERROR GOTO statement.

Answer: The ON ERROR GOTO statement permits the user to intercept and correct errors while the program is in progress. When an error is committed, ON ERROR GOTO transfers control to the appropriate error recovery routine. The ON ERROR GOTO statement is often used in conjunction with the RESUME statement, which, depending on its form, transfers control back to the statement in which the error was committed, to the statement following the statement in which the error was committed, or to another point in the program.

PROBLEM 7-12 The program in Problem 7-8 warns the user not to enter a number larger than 6. However, the program does not ensure that a proper number will be entered. Add a statement to the program in Problem 7-8 to ensure that a value not greater than 6 is entered.

Answer:

```
35 IF N>6 THEN 2Ø
```

If the user enters a number greater than 6, the program will return to line 20, display the message in that line, and request another entry.

PROBLEM 7-13 Given the following program fragment

```
1Ø LET N$="IMA PROGRAMMER"
2Ø LET A$="SAN DIEGO, CA"
3Ø LET P$="555-1212"
```

write a menu subroutine that will provide the following options:

(1) Print the name
(2) Print the address
(3) Print the phone number

Start this subroutine at line 1000 and use an ON . . . GOTO statement.

Answer:

```
1ØØØ REM   THIS IS THE PRINT MENU
1Ø1Ø PRINT "            PRINT MENU"
1Ø2Ø PRINT
1Ø3Ø PRINT "  (1) PRINT THE NAME"
1Ø4Ø PRINT "  (2) PRINT THE ADDRESS"
1Ø5Ø PRINT "  (3) PRINT THE PHONE NUMBER"
1Ø6Ø PRINT
1Ø7Ø PRINT "PLEASE TYPE 1, 2, OR 3 AND HIT <RETURN>"
1Ø8Ø INPUT M
1Ø9Ø IF M<1 OR M>3 THEN 1Ø7Ø
11ØØ ON M GOTO  12ØØ, 13ØØ, 14ØØ
111Ø GOTO 16ØØ
12ØØ PRINT N$
121Ø GOTO 16ØØ
13ØØ PRINT A$
131Ø GOTO 16ØØ
14ØØ PRINT P$
141Ø GOTO 16ØØ
16ØØ RETURN
```

This subroutine displays the following menu:

```
              PRINT MENU

    (1) PRINT THE NAME
    (2) PRINT THE ADDRESS
    (3) PRINT THE PHONE NUMBER

PLEASE TYPE 1, 2, OR 3 AND HIT <RETURN>
```

If the user types 2, for example, line 1080 assigns 2 to M. Line 1090 tests the value of M to determine whether a proper number was entered. The ON . . . GOTO statement in line 1100 transfers control to line 1300, the second line number in the ON . . . GOTO list. Line 1300 then prints the value of A$, which was assigned SAN DIEGO, CA in line 20.

PROBLEM 7-14 Given the program fragment in Problem 7-13, write a menu that lets the user

(1) Input a new name
(2) Input a new address
(3) Input a new phone number

Start this subroutine at line 2000 and use an ON . . . GOSUB statement.

Answer:

```
2000 REM THIS IS THE INPUT MENU
2010 PRINT "            INPUT MENU"
2020 PRINT
2030 PRINT "    (1) INPUT A NEW NAME"
2040 PRINT "    (2) INPUT A NEW ADDRESS"
2050 PRINT "    (3) INPUT A NEW PHONE NUMBER"
2060 PRINT
2070 PRINT "PLEASE TYPE  1, 2, OR 3 AND HIT <RETURN>"
2080 INPUT M
2090 IF M<1 OR M>3 THEN 2070
2100 ON M GOSUB  2200, 2300, 2400
2110 RETURN
2200 INPUT "ENTER THE NEW NAME"; N$
2210 RETURN
2300 INPUT "ENTER THE NEW ADDRESS"; A$
2310 RETURN
2400 INPUT "ENTER THE NEW PHONE NUMBER"; P$
2410 RETURN
```

This subroutine displays the following menu:

```
            INPUT MENU

    (1) INPUT A NEW NAME
    (2) INPUT A NEW ADDRESS
    (3) INPUT A NEW PHONE NUMBER

PLEASE TYPE 1, 2, OR 3 AND HIT <RETURN>
```

If the user types 1, for example, line 2080 assigns 1 to M. Line 2090 tests the value of M, and line 2100 transfers control to line 2200, the first line number in the ON . . . GOTO list. Line 2200 then displays

```
ENTER THE NEW NAME?
```

and the name entered by the user is assigned to N$.

PROBLEM 7-15 Given the subroutines in Problems 7-13 and 7-14, write a subroutine for a main menu that provides the following options:

(1) Display the input menu
(2) Display the print menu
(3) Quit

Answer:

```
100 REM MAIN MENU
110 PRINT "            MAIN MENU"
120 PRINT
130 PRINT "     (1)   INPUT MENU"
140 PRINT "     (2)   PRINT MENU"
150 PRINT "     (3)   QUIT THIS PROGRAM"
160 PRINT
170 PRINT "PLEASE TYPE 1, 2, OR 3 AND HIT <RETURN>"
180 INPUT M
190 IF M<1 OR M>3 THEN 170
200 IF M=3 THEN 10000
210 ON M GOSUB 2000, 1000
220 GOTO 100
10000 END
```

This program displays the following menu:

```
            MAIN MENU

     (1)  INPUT MENU
     (2)  PRINT MENU
     (3)  QUIT THIS PROGRAM

PLEASE TYPE 1, 2, OR 3 AND HIT <RETURN>
```

When 1 or 2 is entered, control transfers to the appropriate subroutine and displays either the input menu or the print menu. After an option in one of those submenus is completed, a RETURN statement in the submenu subroutine returns control to line 220, the line following the ON . . . GOSUB statement. The GOTO statement in line 220 then transfers control back to line 100, and the process can be repeated.

PROBLEM 7-16 The subprograms in Problems 7-13, 7-14, and 7-15 constitute a complete menu-driven program. Notice, however, that the same IF statement is used in each subroutine to test the value of M. Replace these three IF statements with a single subroutine, at the end of the program, that tests the value of M.

Answer:

```
10 LET N$="IMA PROGRAMMER"
20 LET A$="SAN DIEGO, CA"
30 LET P$="555-1212"
100 REM  MAIN MENU
110 PRINT "            MAIN MENU"
120 PRINT
130 PRINT "     (1)   INPUT MENU"
140 PRINT "     (2)   PRINT MENU"
150 PRINT "     (3)   QUIT THIS PROGRAM"
160 GOSUB 3000
200 IF M=3 THEN 10000
210 ON M GOSUB 2000, 1000
220 GOTO 100
1000 REM  THIS IS THE PRINT MENU
```

(continued)

(continued)

```
1010 PRINT "              PRINT  MENU"
1020 PRINT
1030 PRINT "     (1)  PRINT  THE  NAME"
1040 PRINT "     (2)  PRINT  THE  ADDRESS"
1050 PRINT "     (3)  PRINT  THE  PHONE  NUMBER"
1060 GOSUB 3000
1100 ON M GOTO  1200, 1300, 1400
1110 GOTO 1600
1200 PRINT N$
1210 GOTO 1600
1300 PRINT A$
1310 GOTO 1600
1400 PRINT P$
1410 GOTO 1600
1600 RETURN
2000 REM THIS IS THE INPUT MENU
2010 PRINT "              INPUT  MENU"
2020 PRINT
2030 PRINT "     (1)  INPUT  A  NEW  NAME"
2040 PRINT "     (2)  INPUT  A  NEW  ADDRESS"
2050 PRINT "     (3)  INPUT  A  NEW  PHONE  NUMBER"
2060 GOSUB 3000
2100 ON M GOSUB  2200, 2300, 2400
2110 RETURN
2200 INPUT "ENTER THE NEW NAME"; N$
2210 RETURN
2300 INPUT "ENTER THE NEW ADDRESS"; A$
2310 RETURN
2400 INPUT "ENTER THE NEW PHONE NUMBER"; P$
2410 RETURN
3000 REM SUBROUTINE TO VALIDATE INPUT
3010 PRINT
3020 PRINT "PLEASE ENTER 1, 2, OR 3 AND HIT <RETURN>"
3030 INPUT M
3040 IF M<1 OR M>3 THEN 3020
3050 RETURN
10000 END
```

The subroutine that tests the value of M comprises lines 3000 through 3050. To transfer control to this subroutine, GOSUB 3000 is inserted at the appropriate place in each menu subroutine. Line 3050 returns control to the line following the corresponding GOSUB statement.

PROBLEM 7-17 What is wrong with the following program?

```
10 GOSUB 200
20 PRINT "MAIN PROGRAM"
30 INPUT N
40 IF N=0 THEN 1000
50 PRINT N
60 GOTO 10
200 PRINT "SUBROUTINE"
210 GOTO 20
1000 END
```

Answer: This subroutine ends with a GOTO statement at line 210, rather than with a RETURN statement. Whenever a program uses a GOSUB statement to transfer control to a subroutine, the subroutine must use a RETURN statement to transfer control back to the calling program.

PROBLEM 7-18 What is wrong with the following program?

```
10 INPUT N
20 ON N GOTO 100, 200
30 GOTO 1000
100 PRINT "SUBROUTINE 1"
110 RETURN
200 PRINT "SUBROUTINE 2"
210 RETURN
1000 END
```

Answer: The ON . . . GOTO statement is used in conjunction with RETURN statements in lines 110 and 210. Only GOSUB statements can be used with RETURN statements. One remedy is to change line 20 to a GOSUB statement:

```
20 ON N GOSUB 100, 200
```

Another remedy is to change lines 110 and 210 to GOTO statements:

```
110 GOTO 30
210 GOTO 30
```

PROBLEM 7-19 What is wrong with the following program?

```
10 ON ERROR GOTO 70
20 INPUT "FILE NAME"; F$
30 OPEN "0", 1, F$
40 PRINT "THANK YOU FOR A VALID FILE NAME"
50 CLOSE
60 GOTO 90
70 PRINT "FILE NAME IN ERROR"
80 GOTO 20
90 END
```

Answer: If you want the program to continue after an error, replace GOTO 20 in line 80 with RESUME 20.

PROBLEM 7-20 What is the output of the following program when 2 is entered as input?

```
10 INPUT N
20 ON N+6/2*3-10 GOTO 100, 200, 300
100 PRINT "1ST CHOICE"
110 GOTO 1000
200 PRINT "2ND CHOICE"
210 GOTO 1000
300 PRINT "3RD CHOICE"
310 GOTO 1000
1000 END
```

Answer: Substituting 2 for N in line 20, the computer evaluates the expression as follows:

```
2 + ((6/2) * 3) - 10
2 + (3 * 3) - 10
2 + 9 - 10
11 - 10
1
```

Since the value of the expression is 1, the ON . . . GOTO statement transfers control to line 100, the first line number in the ON . . . GOTO list. Consequently, the program will print

```
1ST CHOICE
```

PROBLEM 7-21 What is wrong with the following program?

```
10 INPUT L$
20 ON L$ GOTO 2000,500,3000
500 PRINT "2ND CHOICE"
510 GOTO 10000
2000 PRINT "1ST CHOICE"
2010 GOTO 10000
3000 PRINT "3RD CHOICE"
10000 END
```

Answer: You cannot use a string as the index of an ON . . . GOTO statement. Therefore, ON L$ GOTO is illegal.

PROBLEM 7-22 What is wrong with the following program?

```
10 INPUT "FILE NAME"; F$
20 OPEN "I", 1, F$
30 PRINT "THANK YOU FOR A VALID FILE NAME"
40 CLOSE
50 ON ERROR GOTO 70
60 GOTO 90
70 PRINT "FILE NAME IN ERROR"
80 GOTO 20
90 END
```

Answer: The ON ERROR GOTO statement is useless because it is executed after line 10, which is the line that the ON ERROR GOTO statement is meant to error-trap. Thus, the program will abort when an input error is committed. The ON ERROR GOTO statement should come before any statement or statements that could possibly cause an error.

PROBLEM 7-23 What happens in the following program?

```
10 ON ERROR GOTO 100
20 LET A=5
30 LET B=0
40 LET C=A/B
50 PRINT A; B; C
60 GOTO 2000
100 PRINT "ERROR - DIVIDE BY ZERO"
2000 END
```

Answer: Division by 0 is illegal; therefore, an error occurs in line 40. The ON ERROR GOTO statement transfers control to line 100, which prints an error message. Because the program does not have a RESUME statement, execution terminates after the error message is printed.

PROBLEM 7-24 Insert ON ERROR GOTO statements and RESUME statements where appropriate in the following program.

```
10 INPUT "FILE NAME"; F$
20 OPEN "I", 1, F$
30 PRINT "THANK YOU FOR A VALID FILE NAME"
40 CLOSE
50 INPUT "FILE NAME"; F$
60 OPEN "I", 2, F$
70 PRINT "THANK YOU FOR A VALID FILE NAME"
80 CLOSE
300 END
```

Answer: Add these lines to the program:

```
5 ON ERROR GOTO 100
45 ON ERROR GOTO 200
90 GOTO 300
100 PRINT "FIRST FILE NAME IN ERROR"
110 RESUME 10
200 PRINT "SECOND FILE NAME IN ERROR"
210 RESUME 50
```

PROBLEM 7-25 Write a program for a menu that asks the user choose options by entering Y for "yes," N for "no," and ? for "don't know."

Answer:

```
10 PRINT "TYPE Y FOR YES"
20 PRINT "TYPE N FOR NO"
30 PRINT "TYPE ? FOR DON'T KNOW"
40 PRINT
50 INPUT N$
60 IF N$="Y" THEN 100
70 IF N$="N" THEN 200
80 IF N$="?" THEN 300
90 GOTO 10
100 PRINT "YOU ANSWERED YES"
110 GOTO 1000
200 PRINT "YOU ANSWERED NO"
210 GOTO 1000
300 PRINT "YOU DON'T KNOW THE ANSWER"
1000 END
```

PROBLEM 7-26 Rewrite the program in Problem 7-25 using an ON . . . GOSUB statement.

Answer:

```
10 PRINT "TYPE Y  FOR YES"
20 PRINT "TYPE N  FOR NO"
30 PRINT "TYPE ? FOR DON'T KNOW"
40 PRINT
50 INPUT N$
60 IF N$="Y" THEN GOSUB 200
80 IF N$="N" THEN GOSUB 300
100 IF N$="?" THEN GOSUB 400
110 GOTO 1000
200 PRINT "YOU ANSWERED YES"
210 RETURN
300 PRINT "YOU ANSWERED NO"
```

(continued)

(continued)
```
310  RETURN
400  PRINT "YOU DON'T KNOW THE ANSWER"
410  RETURN
1000 END
```

PROBLEM 7-27 What is wrong with this program?

```
10  PRINT "MAIN PROGRAM"
20  GOSUB 100
30  GOTO 1000
100 PRINT "SUBROUTINE"
110 GOSUB 100
120 RETURN
1000 END
```

Answer: The GOSUB statement in line 110 creates an infinite loop.

PROBLEM 7-28 What is the output of this program?

```
10  FOR J=1 TO 5
20     PRINT J
30     GOSUB 100
40  NEXT J
50  GOTO 1000
100 FOR J=1 TO 10
110    PRINT J
120 NEXT J
130 RETURN
1000 END
```

Answer:

```
1
1
2
3
4
5
6
7
8
9
10
```

Lines 10 and 40 create a loop that is intended to repeat five times. However, after line 20 prints the first value of J (1), the GOSUB statement in line 30 transfers control to another loop, which begins in line 100. This second loop executes ten times, printing the value of J each time. After the loop prints the last value of J (10), the RETURN statement in line 130 returns control to line 40, the last statement in the first loop. However, because the value of J (10) now exceeds the end value (5) of this loop, the loop terminates and control transfers to line 1000, which ends the program.

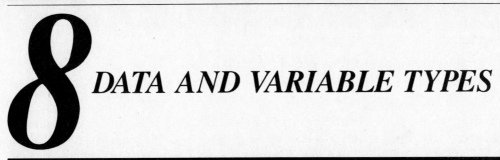

8 DATA AND VARIABLE TYPES

THIS CHAPTER IS ABOUT
☑ **Data Types**
☑ **Variable Types**

8-1. Data Types

Two types of numeric values are commonly used in computer programming: integers and real numbers. *Integers* are used for counting. They are whole numbers; that is, they have no fractional part and do not use a decimal point. *Real numbers* are used for measurement. They can have fractional parts and are written with a decimal point. Many systems also permit the use of *double-precision* real values, which are a variation of real numbers.

Early versions of BASIC did not distinguish between these data types. Since real numbers can represent integer values (such as 1.0 and 42.0), all values were simply stored as real. For example, if the integer 156 were entered as input, BASIC would convert it to 156.0. Today, however, many versions of BASIC permit the use of both integer and real data.

1. Integers are stored in memory in a form that preserves their exact value. Because of this, only small numbers may be used. Most microcomputers permit integers to range from -32768 to $+32767$. Larger computers may allow a greater range. Since integers are whole numbers, any fractional parts will be truncated (discarded).

2. Real numbers are stored in memory in a form that does not necessarily preserve their exact value. This may not be acceptable in financial calculations, which must balance to the penny, but is acceptable in most scientific and engineering calculations, which are assumed to contain some measure of error. Real values have a much greater range than integers. For example, one version of BASIC permits real values to range up to 1.70141×10^{38} (170141 followed by 33 zeros). However, this number can be represented only to a certain number of significant digits of accuracy. (Most systems permit up to 7–9 significant digits for single-precision real values.)

3. Double-precision numbers are a variation of real numbers. Whereas single-precision values may have up to 7–9 significant digits, double-precision values can have twice that many, although the range remains the same as for single precision. This means that double-precision values, both large and small, are more accurate than single-precision values because rounding does not occur until a number exceeds 16 or so significant digits.

EXAMPLE 8-1: If a system permits 7 significant figures for single-precision values, then the number 12865.61987 would be represented as $1.286562E+4$. However, if the system permits double-precision values of up to 16 significant figures, the number would be represented in its original form.

8-2. Variable Types

Many enhanced versions of BASIC permit the use of real, integer, double-precision, and string data values. A given variable may hold one data type only. Since real data are most common, variables are assumed to be real unless otherwise specified. For example, if you assign an integer value to a simple numeric variable, such as X or Y1, BASIC will convert the integer to a real value. In order to save a value in its proper form, the value must be assigned to a variable of the proper type; that is, integers to integer variables, double-precision values to double-precision variables, and string values to string variables.

A. Integer variables are suffixed with a percent sign (%).

On most versions of BASIC, integer variables end with a percent sign. Examples are I%, J1%, and X%(2).

1. On most systems, integer variables occupy less memory than real variables. An integer variable typically occupies two bytes of memory, while a single-precision real variable typically occupies four bytes. In a long program or a program that uses many variables, especially arrays, this difference in memory requirements can become substantial.
2. In general, programs that perform calculations with integers execute faster than programs that perform calculations with real or double-precision values.
3. An integer variable cannot hold fractional values. If a fractional value is assigned to an integer variable, the fractional part will be truncated.

EXAMPLE 8-2: The following program uses the integer variables I% and J1%. However, lines 10 and 20 attempt to assign the real values 2.6 and 3.5 (the quotient of 7 divided by 2) to these variables. The result is that the decimal parts of these numbers are truncated.

```
10 LET I%=2.6
20 LET J1%=7/2
30 PRINT I%, J1%
40 END
```

Display:

```
2            3
```

B. Double-precision variables are suffixed with a pound sign (#).

On most versions of BASIC, double-precision variables end with a pound, or number, sign. Examples are L#, V9#, and G#(2). Increased accuracy and precision are the primary advantages of using double precision. However, double-precision variables use twice as much memory as single-precision variables, and calculations with double-precision values can take much longer than calculations with real or integer values.

EXAMPLE 8-3: The following program assigns 12345.67890123456 to double-precision variable L# and to single-precision variable M. (We are assuming that the computer permits 16 significant digits in double precision and 8 significant digits in single precision.)

```
10 L#=12345.67890123456
20 M=12345.67890123456
30 PRINT L#
40 PRINT M
```

Display:

```
12345.67890123456
12345.679
```

As the displayed output shows, the double-precision variable L# accurately preserves the value assigned to it, but the same value is rounded to eight digits when assigned to the single-precision variable M.

C. String variables are suffixed with a dollar sign ($).

On most versions of BASIC, string variables end with a dollar sign. Examples are D$, Z1$, and B$(7). The value of a string value can be any string of characters or no characters at all (a *null* string). The maximum length of a string varies among versions of BASIC.

EXAMPLE 8-4: The following program assigns the string "Hello" to string variable B$(7) and a null string to string variable Z1$.

```
10 LET B$(7)="Hello"
20 LET Z1$=""
30 PRINT Z1$, B$(7)
```

Display

```
Hello
```

D. Single-precision real variables require no special identification.

As mentioned previously, BASIC will store a value in real form unless explicitly told to do otherwise. No special characters are needed with single-precision real variables; common numeric variables such as I, J1, and X(2) will suffice. However, some versions of BASIC permit you to explicitly declare variables as real. Generally, the exclamation mark is used for this purpose; for example, I!, J1!, X!(2).

RAISE YOUR GRADES

Can you explain . . . ?

☑ the difference between integer and real numbers
☑ the form of integer variables
☑ the difference between single precision and double precision
☑ the form of double-precision variables
☑ an advantage of using integers
☑ the form of string variables
☑ an advantage of using double precision

SUMMARY

1. Two types of numeric values are commonly used in computer programming: integers and real numbers.
2. Integers are whole numbers and are used for counting.
3. Real numbers are decimal numbers and are used for measurement.
4. Integer values are stored in integer variables, which are suffixed with a percent sign (%).
5. An integer variable cannot hold a fractional value. If a fractional value is assigned to an integer variable, the fractional part will be truncated.
6. Integer variables occupy less memory than real variables, usually two bytes as opposed to four bytes.
7. Programs that use integers typically execute faster than programs that use real numbers.
8. BASIC will store a value in real form unless told to do otherwise.
9. Real values have a greater range than integer values.
10. Double-precision is a form of real values with twice the number of significant digits. This makes double precision more accurate than single precision.
11. Double-precision values are stored in double-precision variables, which are suffixed with a pound sign (#).
12. String values are stored in string variables, which are suffixed with a dollar sign ($).
13. Single-precision real variables require no special identification.

RAPID REVIEW   Answers

True or False?

1. Integers have fractional parts and are used for measurement.   False
2. Integer variables occupy less memory than real variables.   True

3. BASIC will implicitly store a value in real form.   True

4. Double precision increases the speed of calculations.   False

5. Double-precision values have twice the range of single-precision
   values.   False

Fill in the blanks

1. J1 is a(n) ＿＿＿＿＿＿ variable.   real

2. K# is a(n) ＿＿＿＿＿＿ variable.   double-precision

3. M% is a(n) ＿＿＿＿＿＿ variable.   integer

4. A single-precision real variable typically occupies ＿＿＿＿＿＿
   bytes of memory.   four

5. String variables are suffixed with a ＿＿＿＿＿＿ sign.   dollar

Multiple choice

1. Which of the following statements will print the value 2.7896436218?

   (*a*) `PRINT X1`   (*c*) `PRINT X#`
   (*b*) `PRINT X`   (*d*) `PRINT X%`   *c*

2. What would be the output of the following program?

   ```
   1Ø LET A%=3.1416
   2Ø PRINT A%
   3Ø END
   ```

   (*a*) `3.1416`   (*b*) `3.1`   (*c*) `3.0`   (*d*) `3`   *d*

3. What would be the output of the following program, assuming
   the system allows 7 significant figures for single-precision values
   and 16 significant figures for double-precision values?

   ```
   1Ø LET Q=165.43219873
   2Ø PRINT Q
   3Ø END
   ```

   (*a*) `165.4321`   (*b*) `165.4322`   (*c*) `1.654321`   (*d*) `165.43219873`   *b*

SOLVED PROBLEMS

PROBLEM 8-1 Briefly explain integer and real values.

Answer: Integers are numbers that are used for counting. They are whole numbers; that is, they have no fractional part and do not use a decimal point. Real numbers are used for measurement. They can have fractional parts and, in BASIC, are written with decimal points. Early versions of BASIC did not distinguish between integer and real values; all values were simply stored as real. Today, many versions of BASIC can manipulate both integer and real values.

PROBLEM 8-2 What is the proper way to store an integer value?

Answer: To properly store an integer value—that is, store it in integer form—you must use an integer variable. An integer variable is suffixed with a percent sign, such as I% and J1%. If you assign an integer value to a simple numeric variable, such as I or J1, BASIC will convert the integer to a real value.

PROBLEM 8-3 What is double precision?

Answer: Double precision is a variation of real values that permits twice the number of significant digits allowed for single-precision real values. Whereas single-precision typically permits values to have up to 7–9 significant digits, double precision typically permits values to have up to 16 significant digits. The advantage of using double precision is that it is more accurate than single precision because rounding occurs at the sixteenth or so significant digit rather than the sixth, seventh, or eighth significant digit.

PROBLEM 8-4 What is the proper way to store a double-precision value?

Answer: To properly store a double-precision value, you must use a double-precision variable. A double-precision variable is suffixed with a pound sign, such as M# and L2#.

PROBLEM 8-5 Write a program that computes and prints the square roots of the numbers 1 through 10 in double precision. (Use the formula $\sqrt{x} = x^{1/2}$ to compute the square roots.)

Answer:

```
10 REM PROGRAM PRINTING SQUARE ROOTS
20 FOR X#=1 TO 10
30 LET Y#=X^0.5
40 PRINT X, Y#
50 NEXT X
60 END
```

PROBLEM 8-6 Write a program that uses integer values to divide one number by another number and then prints the quotient and remainder.

Answer:

```
10 PRINT "ENTER A WHOLE NUMBER: ";
20 INPUT N%
30 PRINT "ENTER THE INTEGER DIVISOR: ";
40 INPUT D%
50 A%=N%/D%
60 R%=N%-(A%*D%)
70 PRINT D%; " GOES INTO "; N%; ", ", A%; " TIMES. ";
80 PRINT "THE REMAINDER IS "; R%
90 GOTO 10
100 END
```

Line 50 divides N by D. Since we are using integer values and variables, the fractional value—if there is one—is truncated. Therefore, we use line 60 to compute the value of the remainder. Lines 70 and 80 print the results.

PROBLEM 8-7 Write a program that computes and prints the product of 3.5486 × 7.9103 in single and double precision. Assume single precision allows 7 significant digits and double precision allows 16.

Answer:

```
10 LET A=3.5486*7.9103
20 LET B#=3.5486*7.9103
30 PRINT A, B#
40 END
```

Display:

```
28.07049    28.07048988342285
```

PROBLEM 8-8 What is the output of the following program?

```
1Ø  D%=Ø
2Ø  D%=D%+1.9
3Ø  PRINT D%
4Ø  IF D%<1Ø THEN 2Ø
5Ø  END
```

Answer:

```
1
2
3
4
5
6
7
8
9
1Ø
```

Since the program uses integer variables, the fractional parts of the numbers are truncated.

PROBLEM 8-9 What is the output of each of these programs?

```
1Ø  LET D#=211/177
2Ø  PRINT D#
3Ø  END
```

```
1Ø  LET D=211/177
2Ø  PRINT D
3Ø  END
```

```
1Ø  LET D%=211/177
2Ø  PRINT D%
3Ø  END
```

Answers:

For the first program: 1.192090392112732
For the second program: 1.19209 (assuming six-digit significance)
For the third program: 1

PROBLEM 8-10 How many bytes of memory does the following array occupy?

```
DIM A%(1ØØØ)
```

Answer: 1001 locations × 2 bytes each = 2,002 bytes. (One integer variable occupies two bytes of memory.)

PROBLEM 8-11 How many bytes of memory does the following array occupy?

```
DIM A(1ØØØ)
```

Answer: 1001 × 4 = 4,004 bytes. (One single-precision variable occupies four bytes of memory.)

PROBLEM 8-12 How many bytes of memory does the following array occupy?

```
DIM A#(1ØØØ)
```

Answer: 1001 × 8 = 8,008 bytes. (One double-precision variable occupies eight bytes of memory.)

PROBLEM 8-13 How many bytes of memory does the following array occupy?

```
DIM A#(1ØØØ, 3)
```

Answer: 1001 × 4 × 8 = 32,032 bytes.

PROBLEM 8-14 Write a dimension statement for an array that is used to record the amount of rainfall to the nearest 1/16th of an inch for every day of a month.

Answer:

```
DIM R(31)
```

You can't use an integer array because the records that are stored in the array have fractional values. Since the fractions are not that precise, you can use a single-precision array rather than a double-precision array.

PROBLEM 8-15 Modify the program in Problem 8-6 so that it prints a message if D% does not divide N% evenly.

Answer: Rewrite lines 70 and 80 as follows:

```
7Ø IF R%=Ø THEN 9Ø
8Ø PRINT D%; " DOES NOT DIVIDE "; N%; " EVENLY"
```

PROBLEM 8-16 Write a program that asks the user to enter an amount between 0 and 99 cents and then prints the correct change for that amount in quarters, dimes, nickels, and pennies. Write the program so that it determines the correct change in the fewest number of coins. For example, if the user enters 79, the program would print

```
3 QUARTERS
Ø DIMES
Ø NICKELS
4 PENNIES
```

Answer:

```
5 REM CHANGE MAKING PROGRAM
1Ø REM Q% IS NUMBER OF QUARTERS, D% IS NUMBER OF DIMES
15 REM F% IS NUMBER OF NICKELS, P% IS NUMBER OF PENNIES
2Ø INPUT "ENTER AN AMOUNT BETWEEN Ø AND 99"; N%
3Ø IF N%<Ø OR N%>99 THEN 2Ø
4Ø LET Q%=N%/25
5Ø LET N%=N%-Q%*25
6Ø LET D%=N%/1Ø
7Ø LET N%=N%-D%*1Ø
8Ø LET F%=N%/5
9Ø LET P%=N%-F%*5
1ØØ PRINT
11Ø PRINT Q%; " QUARTERS"
12Ø PRINT D%; " DIMES"
13Ø PRINT F%; " NICKELS"
14Ø PRINT P%; " PENNIES"
15Ø END
```

Lines 40 through 90 determine the correct change, in the fewest number of coins, for the amount (N%) entered in line 20. Line 40 computes the number of quarters (Q%), lines 50 and 60 compute the number of dimes (D%), lines 70 and 80 compute the number of nickels (F%), and line 90 computes the number of pennies (P%). Lines 110 through 140 print the results.

PROBLEM 8-17 Write a program that determines whether a number is a whole number and then prints the result.

Answer:

```
10 INPUT "PICK A NUMBER, ANY NUMBER"; N
20 LET N%=N
30 IF N=N% THEN 60
40 PRINT N; " IS NOT A WHOLE NUMBER"
50 GOTO 100
60 PRINT N; " IS A WHOLE NUMBER"
100 END
```

Line 10 requests a value for N, and line 20 assigns that value to N%. Since N% is an integer variable, it will truncate any real value assigned to it, making that value a whole number. Line 30 then compares the value of N% to the value of N; this will determine if the value of N is a whole number. If the two values are equal, control transfers to line 60, which prints the appropriate message.

PROBLEM 8-18 What is the output of this program?

```
10 LET A=17
20 LET B=5
30 LET C%=A/5
40 PRINT C%
50 END
```

Answer:

3

Although 17 divided by 5 equals 3.4, the fractional part of the quotient will be truncated when 3.4 is assigned to C% in line 30.

PROBLEM 8-19 Write a program fragment that counts the number of whole numbers in an array A(10) and then prints the result. Assume that the array has already been initialized.

Answer:

```
70 LET C=0
80 FOR J=0 to 10
90 LET T%=A(J)
100 IF T%<>A(J) THEN 120
110 C=C+1
120 NEXT J
130 PRINT
140 PRINT "THERE ARE ";C; " WHOLE NUMBERS IN THE ARRAY"
```

Line 70 initializes C, which will be used to count the number of whole numbers in array A(10). Lines 80 through 120 create a loop that determines the number of whole numbers in A(10). Each repetition of the loop tests each value in the array [A(J)] to determine if that value is a whole number. Line 90 assigns each value of the array to T%, which stores the value as a whole number. Line 100 then tests the value of A(J) against the value of T%. If the value of A(J) is not a whole number, control transfers to line 120 and the loop repeats. If the value of A(J) is a whole number, line 110 increments the counter (C) and the loop then repeats. The loop terminates after the tenth repetition, and line 140 prints the value of C, which is the number of whole numbers in array A(10).

PROBLEM 8-20 You discover that the program fragment in Problem 8-19 exceeds your computer's memory by 4 bytes. How could you revise the program to alleviate this problem?

Answer: Change the real variables C and J to the integer variables C% and J%. This will save 2 bytes of memory for each variable.

PROBLEM 8-21 What is wrong with the following program?

```
1Ø J=Ø.Ø
2Ø PRINT J
3Ø IF J=1.3 THEN 1ØØ
4Ø J=J+Ø.1
5Ø GOTO 2Ø
1ØØ END
```

Answer: The program will never end because the value of J will never equal 1.3. It is not good practice to compare real numbers for equality. We can correct the problem by changing line 30 to

```
3Ø IF J>=1.3 THEN 1ØØ
```

PROBLEM 8-22 What is the output of this program?

```
1Ø LET K%=5
2Ø LET J%=2
3Ø LET T=K%/J%
4Ø PRINT T
5Ø END
```

Answer: This program will print

```
2.5
```

Although the expression in line 30 contains integer variables, the result is assigned to a real variable, which retains the fractional value.

9 FILES AND THE PRINT USING STATEMENT

THIS CHAPTER IS ABOUT

☑ **Sequential and Direct-Access Files**
☑ **Manipulating Files**
☑ **Writing to and Reading from Sequential Files**
☑ **The Structure of Sequential Files**
☑ **Writing to and Reading from Direct-Access Files**
☑ **Formatting Output—the PRINT USING Statement**

9-1. Sequential and Direct-Access Files

A. A *file* is a collection of data.

A fundamental benefit of computers is the ability to quickly and accurately process large quantities of stored data. Most programs are designed to process both user-entered data and existing data stored in data files. A *data file* consists of individual collections of data, called *records*. For example, a personnel file might contain the individual records of 100 employees. Each record might contain an employee's name, wage, and position. Data stored on files may be used over and over again, for many purposes.

B. A *sequential file* contains data stored sequentially.

In a sequential file, data are arranged in sequential order and are read or written in that order. When data are read from a sequential file, reading starts at the beginning of the file and proceeds record by record to the end of the file. Data are written to a sequential file in the same way. BASIC programs may be written to process data from each record in a sequential file or to process data from a specific record only; in each case, however, the file must be read record by record until the desired record is located.

C. A *direct-access file* contains data that can be accessed sequentially or randomly.

In a direct-access file, data may be arranged in sequential or random order; for this reason, direct-access files are also called *random-access files*. Each record in a direct-access file can be located directly, without having to read through every record from the beginning of the file. A record in a direct-access file is identified and accessed by its location in the file.

D. Files are stored primarily on magnetic tape or disk.

Magnetic tape and disk are the most common means of storing data files. The data in the files are encoded on the tape or disk as a series of magnetized spots, which may be changed by erasing old data and writing new data in its place, a method similar to that used for audio tapes. *Storage density* is the amount of data that can be stored on a tape or disk, and *access time* is the speed with which data can be read from or written to the tape or disk.

1. Magnetic computer tape is 1/2 inch wide and usually comes on 2,400-foot reels. A single item of data is recorded in eight magnetized spots (each spot occupies one position on a *track*), across the width of the tape. A ninth track, called a *parity bit*, is used for detecting errors in the data. As many as 6,250 characters may be recorded on an inch of tape; thus tape is extremely useful for storing large amounts of data.

2. There are two major categories of computer disks: "hard" and "floppy." A *hard disk* is an aluminum platter coated with a magnetic surface; it looks something like a phonograph

record. Diameters range from 3 to 20 inches. As with computer tape, data are recorded on hard disks as a series of magnetized spots. In general, hard disks are more durable and can store more data than floppy disks.

The *floppy disk* is usually used on small computer systems because the disks and drives are much less expensive than hard disks. A floppy disk is constructed of slightly flexible plastic with a magnetic coating and is permanently enclosed in a protective envelope. Common diameters are 3 inches, 5 1/4 inches, and 8 inches. For use, the floppy disk is inserted into a *drive*, which has a motor to spin the disk and a read-write head to transfer data to and from the disk.

E. Tape can store only sequential data and files.

Computer tape stores data sequentially, thus it can only store sequential files. This means that data stored on tape must be written and read in sequence from the beginning of the tape, and there is no way to locate a particular record without reading all the preceding records. To change a single record or even a single character, the entire tape must be recopied.

F. Disks can store both direct-access and sequential files.

A computer disk can store both direct (random access) files and sequential files. A disk can hold many files of data, with the location of each file listed in a directory maintained on the disk to provide immediate access to the desired file. Individual files may also have directories, which help locate individual records. The disk is divided into concentric tracks, and as the disk rotates, any single track or part of a track may be read from or written to without having to read other tracks first. This makes it possible to locate a particular record without reading all the other data on the disk. Since it is possible to update individual records by writing new data over old, updating files on disk is much quicker and easier than updating files on tape.

9-2. Manipulating Files

Most versions of BASIC permit the use of both sequential and direct-access files. However, the specific statements that are used to manipulate these files vary considerably according to the version of BASIC being used. You may find, therefore, that your version of BASIC uses statements that differ from those explained here. In general, though, most versions of BASIC use three types of statements to access files for input and output:

1. the OPEN statement prepares a file to be read from or written to
2. input/output statements perform the desired processing
3. the CLOSE statement terminates file input/output processing

The following table shows the specific statements that are typically used to access sequential and direct-access files.

	Sequential	Direct-Access
Open:	OPEN	OPEN
Read from:	INPUT (input)	GET (input)
Write to:	PRINT (output)	PUT (output)
Close:	CLOSE	CLOSE

These statements are discussed in general terms below. They are explained in detail in the sections that follow; in particular, as they relate to sequential and direct files. Although BASIC programs may use tape files, most versions of BASIC are oriented toward disk for both sequential and direct files.

A. The OPEN statement "connects" the file to the program.

Before a file can be accessed for data input or output, it must be "opened." This is accomplished with the OPEN statement. In effect, the OPEN statement "connects" the file to the program; that is, it associates the file with the input/output statements in the program.

The OPEN statement typically performs such functions as verifying that the user has inserted the correct tape or disk for processing, allocating space on disk if a new file is being created, and reserving portions of the computer's memory (called *buffers*) to hold data being read from or written to the files.

The form of the OPEN statement varies among the different versions of BASIC. In Microsoft® BASIC, the form of the OPEN statement is

> OPEN *"mode"*, *n, file name*

In this form of the OPEN statement, *mode* is the letter

"O" to open a sequential file for output from a program
"I" to open a sequential file for input to a program
"R" to open a direct-access (random) file for both input and output

The *n* is a number that the programmer assigns to the file. This number appears in input and output statements and specifies the particular file to access. The *file name* is the name of the file as stored on disk (or tape). Here are three examples of Microsoft® BASIC OPEN statements:

```
1Ø OPEN "I", 1, "INPUT.FIL"
2Ø OPEN "O", 2, "OUTPUT.DAT"
3Ø OPEN "R", 3, "RANDOM"
```

The Microsoft® OPEN statement associates a number with a specific file and indicates how the file will be accessed.

B. An input statement reads data from an opened file.

Some form of input statement must be used in order to read data from an opened file. The type and form of the input statement or statements will vary depending on the version of BASIC being used and whether the file is sequential or direct access.

1. An INPUT statement is typically used to read data from a sequential file. A common form of this statement is

> INPUT *#n, variable 1, variable 2, . . .*

where *#n* is the number assigned to the file in the OPEN statement and the variables are the values to be read from the file. An example is

```
3Ø INPUT #1, X, Y
```

which will obtain two values from file #1. Section 9-3 explains in detail the procedures for reading sequential files.

2. A GET statement is typically used to read data from a direct-access file. A common form of this statement is

> GET *#n, record number*

where *#n* is the number of the file to be read and *record number* specifies the particular record in the file to be read. An example is

```
5Ø GET #2, 5
```

which reads record number 5 from file 2. Section 9-5 explains in detail the procedures for reading direct-access files.

C. An output statement writes data to an opened file.

Some form of output statement must be used in order to write data to an opened file. Again, the type and form of this statement will vary depending on the version of BASIC being used and whether the file is sequential or direct access.

1. A PRINT statement is typically used to write data to a sequential file. A common form of this statement is

> PRINT #*n*, *variable 1*, *variable 2*, . . .

where #*n* is the number of the file to which data are to be written and the variables are the values to be written to the opened file. An example is

```
50 PRINT #1, X, Y
```

Section 9-3 explains in detail the procedures for writing data to sequential files.

2. A PUT statement is typically used to write data to a direct-access file. A common form of this statement is

> PUT #*n*, *record number*

where #*n* is the number of the file to which data are to be written and *record number* specifies the particular record in the file to which the data are to be written. An example is

```
35 PUT #2, 4
```

Section 9-5 explains in detail the procedures for writing data to direct-access files.

D. The CLOSE statement terminates processing of a file.

When a program finishes using a file, the file must then be closed. Most systems automatically close files when the END statement is executed at the end of the program. However, it is better to use a CLOSE statement to explicitly close a file. The CLOSE statement performs several important actions, such as freeing any memory that was used by the file while it was open and updating the disk directory if appropriate. Typical forms of the CLOSE statement are

> CLOSE #*n*

> CLOSE *file name*

where #*n* or *file name*, depending on the version of BASIC you are using, is the file to be closed. An example is

```
80 CLOSE #1
```

9-3. Writing to and Reading from Sequential Files

To write or read sequential files, a BASIC program uses the fundamental three-statement structure described in Section 9-2.

A. Writing data to sequential files

The following example uses Microsoft® BASIC statements to show the proper structure for writing data to a sequential file:

```
1Ø OPEN "O", 1, "AFILE"
2Ø PRINT #1, X, Y, A$
3Ø CLOSE #1
```

Here is a line-by-line explanation of this structure.

1. *An OPEN statement initializes the file.* In the above example, the OPEN statement opens the file AFILE for input or creates the file if it does not already exist. The letter "O" informs the system that this is a sequential output file. The number 1 is assigned as the file number; the output statements that follow the OPEN statement will access the file by this number, not by its name.
2. *The PRINT statement writes data to the file.* The PRINT statement that writes data to a file is similar in form to the standard BASIC PRINT statement (Chapter 3), but also includes the number of the file to which it will write the data. Since the OPEN statement in our example assigned the number 1 to the file AFILE, the PRINT statement also specifies #1. When the PRINT statement is executed, the values of X, Y, and A$ are written to AFILE.
3. *The CLOSE statement completes the data transfer.* The CLOSE statement is used after the last PRINT statement is executed to complete the file processing. If an open file is not properly closed, data may be lost. The reason is that data are not written directly to the file when the PRINT statement is executed; instead, they are stored in a memory buffer until (typically) 128 or 256 bytes are accumulated and then written as a block to the file. The CLOSE statement clears any remaining data from the buffer and transfers it to the disk or tape, and performs any other functions needed to complete the file processing.

B. Reading data from sequential files

The following example uses Microsoft® BASIC statements to show the proper structure for reading data from a sequential file:

```
2Ø OPEN "I", 1, "BFILE"
3Ø INPUT #1, X, Y
4Ø CLOSE #1
```

Here is a line-by-line explanation of this structure.

1. *The OPEN statement initializes the file.* In this example, the OPEN statement opens the file BFILE for sequential input. The file must already exist; otherwise, the program will terminate with an error message, such as FILE NOT FOUND. The letter "I" stands for "input" and informs the system that data will be read into the program from a sequential file. The number 1 is assigned as the file number.
2. *The INPUT statement reads data from the file.* The INPUT statement that reads data from a file is similar in form to the standard INPUT statement that obtains data from the keyboard (Chapter 3), but includes the number of the file from which it will read the data. Since the OPEN statement in our example assigned the number 1 to the file, the INPUT statement also specifies #1. When the INPUT statement is executed, the values X and Y are read from the file.
3. *The CLOSE statement completes data transfer.* The CLOSE statement completes the transfer of data from the file to the program. It also disassociates file #1 from file BFILE so that the file number can be used within the program to access a different file.

9-4. The Structure of Sequential Files

As mentioned earlier, the data stored in sequential files are arranged in a fixed sequence. Within a sequential file, individual data items are separated by characters called *delimiters*. Delimiter characters for numeric data are the space, comma, carriage return, and line feed; the same characters plus the quotation mark are used for string data.

As with keyboard input, the variables in the INPUT list must match the types of data in the file; that is, numeric variables for numeric data and string variables for string data. For example, if a file contains a state name followed by eight numeric values, you would write an INPUT statement with a string variable and eight numeric variables:

```
25 INPUT #2, A$, X1, X2, X3, X4, X5, X6, X7, X8
```

Also, the number of variables in the INPUT list must not exceed the number of data items in the file; for example, if the file contains four data items, the INPUT list must contain no more than four variables.

A. Numeric values and file data

Numeric values are relatively easy to read from or write to sequential files. Simply place the values, separated by commas, in the input or output list; on output, BASIC will separate the values in the file with spaces (or another delimiter) so that a delimiter character appears after each value.

EXAMPLE 9-1: Here are two programs that manipulate numeric values and variables in sequential files. The first program opens EASYFILE for output as file number 2. Lines 20, 30, and 40 assign numeric values to numeric variables. The PRINT statement then writes those values to the file.

```
10 OPEN "O", 2, "EASYFILE"
20 A=21
30 B=32
40 C=45
50 PRINT #2, A, B, C
60 CLOSE #2
70 END
```

BASIC will automatically insert delimiters between the values when they are written. The file will thus contain the characters

```
21□32□45
```

where □ stands for a delimiter (usually a space).

The second program opens EASYFILE for input as file number 3 and reads the three values assigned to the file by the first program. Note that the variables used in this program differ from the variables used in the first program. This is acceptable as long as the variables correspond in type and number. The program then prints the values.

```
10 OPEN "I", 3, "EASYFILE"
20 INPUT #3, J, K, L
30 CLOSE #3
40 PRINT J, K, L
50 END
```

Display:

```
21   32   45
```

B. String values and file data

Writing strings to sequential files is a bit more complicated than writing numbers. The problem is that delimiter characters, such as spaces and commas, are often part of the string. For example, the statement

```
100 PRINT #5, "NIP AND TUCK"
```

would write the characters

```
NIP AND TUCK
```

to the file. Notice that the surrounding quotation marks are not written to the file. If you attempt to read this data with the statement

```
120 INPUT #7, A$
```

only "NIP" would be assigned to A$. The reason is that the space between NIP and AND is a delimiter and thus terminates input. In order to read the entire string, the surrounding quotation marks must also be written to the file, so that the file would contain the data

```
"NIP AND TUCK"
```

By writing the surrounding quotation marks with the characters in this manner, you ensure that string data will be read as intended.

1. One way to write string data with surrounding quotation marks is to use the function CHR$(34). This function produces a quotation mark. Placing CHR$(34) on both sides of a string in a PRINT statement list will surround the string with quotation marks on the file.
2. In many versions of BASIC, when several strings are written to a file, they must be separated by commas. To write these commas to the file, you simply place them in quotation marks in the PRINT statement.

EXAMPLE 9-2: The following program shows how the CHR$(34) function can be used to write strings and their quotation marks to a file.

```
10 LET F$="FIRST STRING, SECOND STRING, "
20 LET L$=" LAST STRING. "
30 OPEN "O", 1, "SOME.TXT"
40 PRINT #1,CHR$(34);F$;CHR$(34);",";CHR$(34);L$;CHR$(34)
50 CLOSE #1
60 OPEN "I", 1, "SOME.TXT"
70 INPUT #1, A$, B$
80 CLOSE #1
90 PRINT A$; B$
100 END
```

Display:

```
FIRST STRING, SECOND STRING, LAST STRING.
```

Lines 10 and 20 assign the strings to variables F$ and L$. Line 30 opens the file SOME.TXT. In the print statement list (line 40), CHR$(34) functions are placed on both sides of the string variables; this will cause the quotation marks in the string to be written to the file. Notice the position of the comma; the quotation marks will cause it to be written to the file between the F$ string and the L$ string in the file.

EXAMPLE 9-3: It's tedious to use CHR$(34) each time you need a quotation mark, and confusing to see the comma in quotes. The following program shows how to overcome these inconveniences.

```
5 Q$=CHR$(34)
6 C$=","
10 F$="FIRST STRING, SECOND STRING, "
20 L$=" LAST STRING. "
30 OPEN "O", 1, "SOME.TXT"
40 PRINT #1, Q$; F$; Q$; C$; Q$; L$; Q$
```

This program assigns CHR$(34) to Q$ and " , " to C$. Q$ and C$ can then be used in place of CHR$(34) and " , " in the PRINT list.

9-5. Writing to and Reading from Direct-Access Files

As mentioned in Section 9-1, direct-access files store data in random order. This permits data to be read from or written to the file directly, without sequentially accessing the entire contents of the file. The data in a direct-access file are organized into records of uniform length, and each record may be read in part or in whole.

A. The locations of direct-access records are numbered.

Although records in a direct-access file are accessed randomly, their locations in the file are numbered sequentially from the beginning of the file. The location numbers usually begin at 1 and proceed up to a maximum number that is specified by the system. Each record in a direct-access file is identified and accessed by its location number.

B. BASIC maintains a pointer for accessing direct-access records.

BASIC uses a pointer to indicate which record in a direct-access file is to be accessed. When a file is opened, the pointer is automatically set to the first record in the file. After each record is accessed, the pointer is set to the next record. BASIC will continue to set the pointer in this manner unless the program specifies that the pointer is to be set to certain records. Thus a direct-access file may be accessed sequentially by simply allowing BASIC to increment the pointer. However, changing the value of the pointer permits you to access records in any order desired.

C. An OPEN statement opens a direct-access file for input and output.

A direct-access file is opened with an OPEN statement. The OPEN statement identifies the file as direct access, specifies a file number, which is used for communication between the program and the file, and lists the file name. Here is an example:

```
35 OPEN "R", 1, "RANDFILE"
```

R identifies the file as direct (random) access; 1 is the number assigned to the file *buffer*; and RANDFILE is the name of the file. Only one form of OPEN statement is needed to open a direct-access file for input, output, or both. This differs from sequential files, which require different OPEN statements: OPEN "I" for input and OPEN "O" for output.

1. In direct-access files, data are not assigned directly to variables. Instead, the OPEN statement assigns an area of memory called a file buffer to each file. The buffer holds a single record. During output, the program fills the buffer with data and then copies the buffer into a record in the file. During input, a record is read into the buffer from the file and the contents of the buffer are then assigned to variables in the program.

2. The buffer is divided into *fields* of various names and lengths. This is done with a FIELD statement, which specifies the name and length of each field in a buffer. The FIELD statement is executed after the file is opened but before it is read from or written to. Here is an example of a FIELD statement:

```
15 FIELD #1, 3Ø AS LNAME$, 28 AS FNAME$, 198 AS REST$
```

FIELD #1 associates the field specifications with file buffer #1. 30 AS LNAME$ creates a field called LNAME$ that is 30 characters long; 28 AS FNAME$ creates a field called FNAME$ that is 28 characters long; REST$ is 198 characters long. The total number of characters (bytes) specified by the fields in a buffer must add up to the number of bytes in a record. In this case, we are assuming that each record is 256 bytes long.

3. Field names are similar in form to string variable names and are usually subject to the same rules that are used for naming strings.

D. A CLOSE statement closes a direct-access file.

A direct-access file is closed in the same manner as a sequential file: with a CLOSE statement. A CLOSE statement with a file number closes only the specified file. For example,

```
50 CLOSE #1
```

closes file #1. In some versions of BASIC a CLOSE statement without a file number closes all open files, whether direct or sequential.

E. Writing data to a direct-access file

Once a direct-access file has been opened and the buffer fields have been specified, the file is ready to receive data. Unlike sequential files, direct-access files only store string data. This means that string values can be transferred directly into the buffer and then to the file, but numeric values must first be converted to strings.

1. *Writing string values to a direct-access file.* Writing strings to a direct-access file is a two-step process involving two types of statements. First, the string must be transferred from the program to the buffer. This is done with an LSET statement or an RSET statement. Second, the data must be transferred from the buffer to the file. This is done with a PUT statement.

    • LSET places a string in the leftmost portion of a field. For example, if an LSET statement places a five-character string in a ten-byte field, the string will occupy the first five positions of the field while the remaining five positions will be blank.
    • RSET places a string in the rightmost portion of a field. For example, if an RSET statement places a seven-character string in a twenty-character field, the string will occupy the last seven positions of the field while the first thirteen positions will be blank.
    • The PUT statement transfers the data in the buffer to a record in the file assigned to that buffer. The PUT statement must specify the number of the buffer. It may also specify the number of a certain record. For example,

```
15 PUT #1, 4
```

transfers the contents of file buffer #1 to record 4 of the appropriate file. If no record number is specified, then the buffer is written to the current record. When the file is first opened, the current record is the first record in the file. As each record is accessed, the next record becomes the current record. For example,

```
40 PUT #3
```

transfers the contents of file buffer #3 to the current record of the appropriate file.

EXAMPLE 9-4: The following program shows how string data are written to a direct-access file.

```
10 OPEN "R", 1, "ANYFILE"
20 FIELD #1, 12 AS LASTNAME$, 244 AS REST$
30 A$="SMITH"
40 B$="JONES"
50 RSET LASTNAME$=A$
60 PUT #1, 1
70 LSET LASTNAME$=B$
80 PUT #1, 2
90 CLOSE
100 END
```

Line 10 opens the direct-access file ANYFILE and assigns buffer 1 to it. Line 20 divides the buffer into two fields: LASTNAME$, which is 12 bytes long, and REST$, which is 244 bytes long.

Line 30 assigns the string "SMITH" to string variable A$, and line 40 assigns the string "JONES" to string variable B$. In line 50, RSET places the value of A$ in the rightmost portion of field LASTNAME$, leaving the first seven positions blank. Line 60 then transfers the contents of LASTNAME$ to the first record in the file. In line 70, LSET places the value of B$ in the leftmost portion of LASTNAME$, leaving the remaining seven positions blank. Line 80 then transfers the contents of LASTNAME$ to the second record in the file. Line 90 closes the file, and line 100 ends the program.

2. *Writing numeric values to a direct-access file.* Writing numeric values to a direct-access file is a three-step process. First, the numeric value must be converted to a string. Second, the string must be transferred from the program to the buffer; this is done by using an LSET or RSET statement. Third, the data must be transferred from the buffer to the file by using a PUT statement.

- Three functions are typically available to convert numeric values to strings. MKI$($x$) converts an integer value to a two-byte string value; the value of the argument (x) must be between -32768 and 32767 (on most systems). MKS$($x$) converts a single-precision real value to a four-byte string value. MKD$($x$) converts a double-precision real value to an eight-byte value.
- Each numeric value that you store in a direct-access file will occupy two, four, or eight bytes, depending on whether the value is integer, single precision, or double precision. When you set up the buffer fields, you should reserve exactly the amount of space needed for the values you are using.

EXAMPLE 9-5: The following program stores name (string value), age (integer value), and salary (single-precision value) data in direct-access file NAMEFILE.

```
10 OPEN "R", 3, "NAMEFILE"
20 FIELD #3, 12 AS NAME$, 2 AS AGE$, 4 AS SALARY$, 238 AS REST$
30 INPUT "Name, age, salary"; N$, A%, S
40 LSET NAME$=N$
50 LSET AGE$=MKI$(A%)
60 LSET SALARY$=MKS$(S)
70 PUT #3, 1
80 CLOSE
100 END
```

Notice that the field statement (line 20) reserves two bytes for AGE$ (A%), which is an integer variable, and four bytes for SALARY (S), which is a single-precision variable. Function MKI$ in line 50 converts integer A% to a two-byte string. Function MKS$ in line 60 converts single-precision S to a four-byte string.

F. Reading data from a direct-access file

The procedure for reading data from a direct-access file is the reverse of the procedure used for writing data to a direct-access file. First, the record must be transferred from the file to the buffer; this is done with a GET statement. Then the record must be transferred from the buffer to the program; this is done with various statements, often PRINT and assignment statements.

1. The GET statement transfers data from the file to the buffer assigned to that file. The GET statement must specify the number of the buffer. It may also specify the number of a certain record. For example,

```
25 GET #1, 3
```

transfers record 3 from the file to buffer #1. If no record is specified, then the default record is transferred to the buffer.

2. Once a record has been transferred from the file to the buffer, it can then be read and used by the program much like any ordinary string variable if its contents are string data. Remember, however, that only strings can be stored in direct-access files and that numeric data must be converted to string form in order to be stored in a direct-access file. This means that the numeric data stored in string form in the file must be converted back to numeric form when transferred from the file to the program. This is accomplished by three functions: CVI, CVS, CVD.

- CVI is the opposite of MKI$. Whereas MKI$ converts an integer value to a two-byte string, CVI converts the integer stored as a two-byte string back to its numeric form.
- CVS is the opposite of MKS$. Whereas MKS$ converts a single-precision real value to a four-byte string, CVS converts the single-precision real value stored as a four-byte string back to its numeric form.
- CVD is the opposite of MKD$. Whereas MKD$ converts a double-precision real value to an eight-byte string, CVD converts the double-precision real value stored as an eight-byte string back to its numeric form.

EXAMPLE 9-6: The program in Example 9-5 showed how name, age, and salary data could be stored in a direct-access file. Here is the same program modified to retrieve the data written to the file and then print that information.

```
1Ø OPEN "R", 3, "NAMEFILE"
2Ø FIELD #3, 12 AS NAME$, 2 AS AGE$, 4 AS SALARY$, 238 AS REST$
3Ø INPUT "Name, age, salary"; N$, A%, S
4Ø LSET NAME$=N$
5Ø LSET AGE$=MKI$(A%)
6Ø LSET SALARY$=MKS$(S)
7Ø PUT #3, 1
8Ø GET #3, 1
9Ø PRINT "Name: "; NAME$
1ØØ PRINT "Age: "; CVI(AGE$)
11Ø PRINT "Salary $"; CVS(SALARY$)
12Ø CLOSE
13Ø END
```

Display:

```
Name, age, salary? Edwards, 31, 5Ø4ØØ
Name: Edwards
Age: 31
Salary: $5Ø4ØØ
```

Lines 10 through 70 of this program are the same as lines 10 through 70 of the program in Example 9-5. Line 10 opens the file, line 20 sets up the buffer fields, line 30 receives input for three values, lines 40 through 60 assign these values to specific fields (lines 50 and 60 convert numeric values to strings), and line 70 writes the values in the fields to record 1 in the file. The GET statement (line 80) retrieves the values from record 1 and places them in the buffer. Line 90 prints the value assigned to field NAME$; since this value was originally a string, it can be printed in the same form in which it is stored in the buffer. Line 100 prints the value assigned to field AGE$. Notice, however, that we must use the function CVI to convert the value back to its numeric form (integer). Line 110 prints the value assigned to field SALARY$; CVS converts the value back to its numeric form (single precision).

9-6. Formatting Output—the PRINT USING Statement

The standard PRINT statement, while useful, provides little control of the output format. To overcome this deficiency, many versions of BASIC offer a PRINT USING statement. The PRINT

USING statement permits the programmer to specify the format of printed output, both for numbers and for strings.

A. The form of the PRINT USING statement

The form of the PRINT USING statement is

> PRINT USING *format string; variable list*

The *format string* is a structural representation of the format that the printed output will take. This string consists of certain characters that specify the output format of the values in the variable list. The output format is often called the *field*, so the format string is often called the *field specification*.

EXAMPLE 9-7: The following program uses a PRINT USING statement to format the output of the value assigned to variable B.

```
10 B=14.37
20 PRINT USING "###.##"; B
30 END
```

Display:

```
14.37
```

In this program, ###.## is the format string, often called a *field specification*. This string specifies that the number to be printed will have a decimal point followed by two digits. Had we used a value with only one digit following the decimal point, such as 14.3, the PRINT USING statement would have assigned a zero to the second decimal position, and the display would have been

```
14.30
```

B. The PRINT USING format string uses certain characters to specify output format.

The PRINT USING statement uses certain characters in the format string to specify the format of the output. On most systems, these characters are

$$\# \ \$ \ * \ - \ + \ \wedge \ \backslash \ ! \ , \ .$$

Some versions of BASIC use other characters, such as % instead of \. Be sure to check the version of BASIC you are using for the specific characters that may be used in the format string.

1. The number sign (#) is used to specify the format for numeric values. Each # in the format string stands for a numeric digit, and commas and decimal points may also be used. Example 9-7 shows how this character is used.
2. A single dollar sign ($) at the beginning of a numeric format string prints a dollar sign at that position. For example,

```
20 PRINT USING "$####.##"; 25.75
```

will print

```
$  25.75
```

with two spaces between the dollar sign and the value. Placing two dollar signs at the beginning of a numeric format string will print a "floating" dollar sign; that is, a dollar sign whose position is not fixed but "floats" so that the dollar sign will be adjacent to the numeric value, regardless of the number of digits in the value. For example,

```
30 PRINT USING "$$####.##"; 54.58
```

will print

```
$54.58
```

3. Two asterisks (**) at the beginning of a numeric format string will fill all the unoccupied positions to the left of the value with asterisks. This is called *asterisk fill*. For example,

```
20 PRINT USING "*###,###.##"; 148.40
```

will print

```
*********148.40
```

4. Two asterisks followed by a dollar sign (**$) at the beginning of a format string will float the dollar sign and print asterisks in the preceding spaces. For example,

```
20 PRINT USING "**$##,###,###.##"; 542.75
```

will print

```
*********$542.75
```

This technique is often used for printing checks because the asterisks make it difficult for anyone to alter the amount printed on the check.

5. A minus sign (−) to the right of the numeric format string prints a minus sign in that position if the value is negative. If the value is positive, no sign will be printed. For example,

```
40 PRINT USING "###.##-"; -46.23
```

will print

```
46.23-
```

Had the number been positive, the statement would have printed

```
46.23
```

6. A plus sign (+) either to the right or the left of a numeric format string prints a plus sign if the value is positive or a minus sign if the value is negative. For example,

```
40 PRINT USING "+###.##"; 46.23
```

will print

```
+46.23
```

Had the number been negative, the statement would have printed

```
-46.23
```

7. Four carets (^^^^) at the end of a numeric format string specify exponential format. These carets will print E + *xx* or E − *xx* in single precision, or D + *xx* or D − *xx* in double precision. For example,

```
35 PRINT USING "##.##^^^^"; 89342.8
```

will print (in single precision)

```
8.93E+04
```

8. Two backslashes (\ \) are used to specify the format for strings. For example,

```
40 PRINT USING "\ \"; "HELLO"
```

will print

```
HELLO
```

The number of positions in the format string, including the slashes, must be the same as the number of characters in the string value to be printed. If the number of characters in the string value is greater than the number of positions in the format string, only the leftmost characters will be printed. If the string value has fewer positions than the number of positions in the format string, all the characters will be printed at the left of the string.

9. An exclamation mark (!) is used to print the first character of a string value. For example,

```
30 PRINT USING "!"; "ICU"
```

will print

```
I
```

C. The format string may be assigned to a variable.

It is often useful to assign a format string to a variable and then use that variable in subsequent PRINT USING statements. This permits you to use the same format string in several PRINT USING statements without having to rewrite the string in each statement.

EXAMPLE 9-8: The following program shows how a format string may be assigned to a variable and then used in a PRINT USING statement.

```
10 INPUT "WHAT IS THE PRICE"; ;P$
20 B$="$$###.##"
30 PRINT USING B$; P$
40 END
```

Display:

```
WHAT IS THE PRICE? 14.82
$14.82
```

Line 10 asks the user to enter a price (P$). Line 20 assigns a format string to B$. The PRINT USING statement in line 30 then prints the value of P$ according to the format string assigned to B$.

RAISE YOUR GRADES

Can you explain . . . ?

☑ the difference between a sequential file and a direct-access file
☑ what type of file may be stored on tape
☑ what type of file may be stored on disk
☑ the purpose of the OPEN statement
☑ the purpose of the CLOSE statement
☑ how data are written to and read from a sequential file
☑ how data are written to and read from a direct-access file
☑ the purpose of the FIELD statement
☑ the purpose of the PRINT USING statement
☑ how the various characters in the PRINT USING format string are used

SUMMARY

1. In BASIC, a file is a collection of data.
2. A sequential file contains data stored in sequential order. The file must be read from or written to sequentially, from the beginning of the file to the end.
3. A direct-access, or random, file contains data that can be accessed sequentially or randomly. Each record can be read from or written to directly; the program does not have to scan the entire file from beginning to end.
4. Sequential files may be stored on magnetic tape or disk, while direct-access files must be stored on disk.
5. Before a file can be used, it must be opened. This is done with an OPEN statement.
6. Once a file is open, it can be used for input or output of data. A file is opened for input when data are to be read by a program. A file is opened for output when data are to be written from a program to the file.
7. A sequential file may be opened for either input or output but not both at the same time. A direct-access file may be opened for both input and output.
8. Statements used for data input include the INPUT statement (for sequential files) and the GET statement (for direct-access files). Statements used for data output include the PRINT statement (for sequential files) and the PUT statement (for direct-access files).
9. When a program completes its processing of a file, the file must then be closed. This is done with a CLOSE statement.
10. Within a sequential file, individual data items are separated by characters called delimiters. On most systems, delimiters for numeric data are the space, comma, carriage return, and line feed. These same characters plus the quotation mark are used for string data.
11. The locations of the records in a direct-access file are numbered, and each record is accessed by its location number.
12. A file buffer acts as an intermediary between a direct-access file and a program. A FIELD statement divides the buffer into fields of various names and lengths.
13. The LSET statement places a string in the leftmost portion of a buffer field. The RSET statement places a string in the rightmost portion of a buffer field.
14. Only strings can be written to a direct-access file. To write a numeric value to a direct-access file, the value must first be converted to a string. Three functions are used for this purpose: MKI\$; MKS\$, and MKD\$. Three functions are also used to convert the string back to a numeric value for input to the program; these functions are CVI, CVS, and CVD.
15. The PRINT USING statement permits the programmer to specify the format of the printed output, both for numbers and for strings.

16. The PRINT USING statement uses certain characters in the format string to specify the output format. On most systems, these characters are

$$\# \quad \$ \quad * \quad - \quad + \quad \wedge \quad \backslash \quad ! \quad , \quad .$$

RAPID REVIEW   Answers

True or False?

1. A sequential file is also called a random file.   False
2. Direct files must be stored on magnetic tape.   False
3. A direct-access file can store data sequentially or randomly.   True
4. An input statement writes data to an opened file.   False

Fill in the blanks

1. A(n) _____ statement is typically used to read data from a sequential file.   INPUT

2. A(n) _____ statement is typically used to read data from a direct-access file.   GET

3. A(n) _____ statement is typically used to write data to a sequential file.   PRINT

4. A(n) _____ statement is typically used to write data to a direct-access file.   PUT

5. The function _____ converts an integer value to a two-byte string value.   MKI$

Multiple choice

1. Each record in a direct-access file is identified and accessed by its

   (*a*) name   (*c*) location number
   (*b*) field number   (*d*) length   *c*

2. A file buffer is the same length as a

   (*a*) field   (*c*) file
   (*b*) record   (*d*) byte   *b*

3. Which function converts a single-precision real value to a four-byte string?

   (*a*) MKD$ (*c*) CHR$
   (*b*) CVS   (*d*) MKS$ *d*

4. Which of the following statements will print a floating dollar sign?

   (*a*) 2Ø PRINT USING "$$###.##"; B$
   (*b*) 2Ø PRINT USING "**###.##"; B$
   (*c*) 2Ø PRINT USING "$###.##"; B$
   (*d*) 2Ø PRINT USING "$+###.##"; B$ *a*

5. What would be the output of the following statement?

   ```
   4Ø PRINT USING "$+###.##"; -24.75
   ```

   (*a*) $24.75   (*c*) $ 24.75
   (*b*) $ -24.75   (*d*) $-24.75   *d*

SOLVED PROBLEMS

PROBLEM 9-1 Explain what happens in the following program.

```
10 OPEN "O", 1, "DATFILE"
20 READ W,X,Y,Z
30 PRINT #1, W,X,Y,Z
40 CLOSE #1
50 DATA 15, 21, 84, 11
60 END
```

Answer: Line 10 opens for output the sequential file DATFILE and assigns file number 1 to it. Line 20 reads values for variables W, X, Y, and Z from the DATA statement in line 50. Line 30 writes the values of W, X, Y, and Z to DATFILE. Line 40 closes the file, and line 60 ends the program.

PROBLEM 9-2 What is wrong with the following program?

```
10 OPEN "I", 1, "DATFILE"
20 PRINT #1, X, Y
30 CLOSE #1
40 END
```

Answer: Line 10 opens the sequential file DATFILE for input to the program. However, the PRINT statement in line 20 will attempt to write data from the program to the file. To correct this problem, we could either revise line 10 so that it opens the file for output (replacing "I" with "O") or replace line 20 with an INPUT statement.

PROBLEM 9-3 What would be the output of the following statement?

```
25 PRINT USING "My car cost $########."; 9500
```

Answer: This statement would print

```
My car cost $     9500.
```

To close up the space between the $ and 9500, we would use two dollar signs in the format string to create a floating dollar sign:

```
25 PRINT USING "My car cost $$########."; 9500
```

This statement would print

```
My car cost $9500.
```

PROBLEM 9-4 Write a program that will read the values 24, 3, 4.15, and 3098 into the variables A, B1, C8, and D and will then write these values to the sequential file NEWFILE. Use file number 3.

Answer:

```
10 OPEN "O", 3, "NEWFILE"
20 READ A, B1, C8, D
30 PRINT #3, A, B1, C8, D
```

(continued)

(continued)
```
40 CLOSE #3
50 DATA 24, 3, 4.15, 3098
60 END
```

Line 10 opens NEWFILE for output and assigns file number 3 to it. Line 20 reads values for variables A, B1, C8, and D from the DATA statement in line 50. Line 30 writes the values of A, B1, C8, and D to NEWFILE. Line 40 closes the file, and line 60 ends the program.

PROBLEM 9-5 Write a program that will read the first three values from sequential file OLDFILE and will then print these values. Use file number 2.

Answer:

```
10 OPEN "I", 2, "OLDFILE"
20 INPUT #2, X, Y, Z
30 CLOSE #2
40 PRINT X, Y, Z
50 END
```

Line 10 opens OLDFILE for input and assigns file number 2 to it. Line 20 reads the first three values from the file and assigns them to variables X, Y, and Z. Line 30 closes the file, and line 40 prints the values of X, Y, and Z.

PROBLEM 9-6 Write a program that prints six 3-digit numbers, with each number preceded by five asterisks.

Answer:

```
10 READ N
20 PRINT USING "**######"; N
30 GOTO 10
40 DATA 325, 123, 727, 969, 733, 579
50 END
```

The double asterisks in the PRINT USING statement specify asterisk fill and will place asterisks in the five unoccupied spaces to the left of each value.

PROBLEM 9-7 Write a program with a PRINT USING statement that will produce the following output:

```
    -4.35
+3,900.40
   +421.01
+6,011.20
```

Answer:

```
10 READ A
20 PRINT USING "+#,###.##"; A
30 GOTO 10
40 DATA -4.35, 3900.4, 421.01, 6011.2
50 END
```

The plus sign at the left in the format string prints a plus sign or a minus sign at the left of each number, depending on the number's value.

PROBLEM 9-8 What would be the output of the following program?

```
1Ø  READ B
2Ø  PRINT USING "###.##+"; B
3Ø  GOTO 1Ø
4Ø  DATA -2ØØ.3, -6Ø.5, 1ØØ, 24.1
5Ø  END
```

Answer:

```
2ØØ.3Ø-
 6Ø.5Ø-
1ØØ.ØØ+
 24.1Ø+
```

The plus sign at the right in the format string prints a plus sign or a minus sign at the right of each number, depending on the number's value.

PROBLEM 9-9 What is the output of the following program?

```
1Ø  FOR I=6 TO 12
2Ø  PRINT USING "##.##"; I;
3Ø  NEXT I
4Ø  END
```

Answer:

```
 6.ØØ 7.ØØ 8.ØØ 9.ØØ1Ø.ØØ11.ØØ12.ØØ
```

The program leaves a space between 6.00, 7.00, 8.00, and 9.00 because the leftmost # in the format string is unoccupied. However, when the value of I reaches 10, each # is filled, thus eliminating the space between the numbers.

PROBLEM 9-10 Write a program with a PRINT USING statement that prints the following:

```
$28.5Ø
$39.22
$17.42
$12.98
------
$98.12
```

Answer:

```
 5  LET X=Ø
1Ø  READ P
2Ø  IF P=-1 THEN 6Ø
3Ø  PRINT USING "$##.##";P
4Ø  LET X=X+P
5Ø  GOTO 1Ø
6Ø  PRINT "------"
7Ø  PRINT USING "$##.##"; X
8Ø  DATA 28.5Ø, 39.22, 17.42, 12.98, -1
9Ø  END
```

Line 5 initializes X. Line 10 reads values for P. Line 20 tests the value of P; if P is −1, then the loop in lines 10–50 terminates and control transfers to line 60. Line 30 specifies the print format for P. Line 40 adds each value of P as it is read and stores the result in X. Line 50 returns control to line 10. Line 60 prints a line following the last value of P. Line 70 specifies the print format for

X. Line 80 provides the data for P; the −1 at the end of the data line is used to terminate the loop in lines 10–50.

PROBLEM 9-11 Write a statement in Microsoft® BASIC to open the sequential file CONCOR.DAT for input. Use disk drive A and channel 2.

Answer:

```
10 OPEN "I", 2, "A:CONCOR.DAT"
```

PROBLEM 9-12 Write a statement in Microsoft® BASIC to open the sequential file NEWFILE.TXT for output, on the default disk drive, using channel number 12.

Answer:

```
10 OPEN "O", 12, "NEWFILE.TXT"
```

PROBLEM 9-13 Write a statement in Microsoft® BASIC to open a random-access file RAND-FILE on disk drive B, using buffer 9.

Answer:

```
10 OPEN "R", 9, "B:RANDFILE"
```

PROBLEM 9-14 What is wrong with the following program?

```
10 OPEN "I", 1, "FILE1"
20 OPEN "I", 1, "FILE2"
30 INPUT #1, X,Y
40 PRINT X,Y
50 CLOSE
60 END
```

Answer: In line 20, the program tries to open FILE2 using channel #1, but channel #1 has already been assigned to FILE1. A channel may be associated with only one file at a time.

PROBLEM 9-15 Write a program that opens two files, FILE1 and FILE2, reads a number from each file, and prints the sum of the two numbers.

Answer:

```
10 OPEN "I", 1, "FILE1"
20 OPEN "I", 2, "FILE2"
30 INPUT #1, X
40 INPUT #2, Y
50 PRINT X+Y
60 CLOSE
70 END
```

PROBLEM 9-16 The file STUDENT.DAT contains the following data.

Student #	Quiz Score	Exam Score	Grade
1	10	97.5	"A"
2	7	85.0	"B"
3	5	51.5	"D"
−1	−1	−1	""

Write a program that reads each set of scores from the file and then prints them.

Answer:

```
10 OPEN "I", 1, "STUDENT. DAT"
20 INPUT #1, I%, Q%, E, G$
30 IF I%=-1 THEN 60
40 PRINT I%, Q%, E, G$
50 GOTO 20
60 CLOSE #1
70 END
```

Line 10 opens the file and line 20 reads the data from the file. Notice the types of variables used in the INPUT statement. I% and Q% are integer variables that store integer data; E is a real variable that stores real data; and G$ is a string variable that stores string data. Line 30 terminates input when the end of the file is reached. Line 40 prints the values stored in the variables.

PROBLEM 9-17 Using the file STUDENT.DAT, write a program that inputs the values from that file and prints the exam scores of all the students who received an A.

Answer:

```
10 OPEN "I", 2, "STUDENT. DAT"
20 INPUT #2, I%, Q%, E, G$
30 IF I%=-1 THEN 60
40 IF G$="A" THEN PRINT E
50 GOTO 20
60 CLOSE #2
70 END
```

Notice that we still have to input all four values, I%, Q%, E, and G$, even though we're interested only in the exam score and the grade.

PROBLEM 9-18 Rewrite the program in Problem 9-17 so that it writes the exam scores to a file REPORT on disk drive A.

Answer: The modified lines are

```
5 OPEN "O", 1, "A: REPORT"
40 IF G$="A" THEN PRINT #1, E
60 CLOSE
```

PROBLEM 9-19 Write a program that creates the file STUDENT.DAT and receives its input from the user at the keyboard.

Answer:

```
10 OPEN "O", 1, "STUDENT. DAT"
20 Q$=CHR$(34)
30 C$=", "
40 INPUT "ENTER STUDENT #", I%
50 INPUT "ENTER QUIZ SCORE", Q%
60 INPUT "ENTER EXAM SCORE", E
70 INPUT "ENTER LETTER GRADE", G$
80 PRINT #1, I%; C$; Q%; C$; E; C$; Q$; G$; Q$
90 IF I%<> -1 THEN 40
100 CLOSE #1
110 END
```

Lines 20, 30, and 80 preserve the commas and quotes in the file STUDENT.DAT.

PROBLEM 9-20 Why is CHR$(34) used to define a quote mark?

Answer: Since quote marks are used to delimit a string, a string of one quote would be """. However, most versions of BASIC will match the second quote with the first one, thus forming an empty string and leaving an extra quote mark. CHR$(34) lets us specify a one-character string without using quotes at all.

PROBLEM 9-21 Rewrite the program in Problem 9-16 to read from the random-access file, STUDENT2.DAT.

Answer:

```
10 OPEN "R", 1, "STUDENT2.DAT"
20 FIELD #1, 2 AS I1$, 2 AS Q1$, 4 AS E1$, 1 AS G1$
30 GET #2
40 IF CVI(I1$)=-1 THEN 70
50 PRINT CVI(I1$), CVI(Q1$), CVS(E1$), G1$
60 GOTO 30
70 CLOSE #1
80 END
```

PROBLEM 9-22 Modify the program in Problem 9-21 so that it prints the records in reverse order. Assume there are 3 records in the file.

Answer:

```
10 OPEN "R", 1, "STUDENT2.DAT"
20 FIELD #1, 2 AS I1$, 2 AS Q1$, 4 AS E1$, 1 AS G1$
25 J%=3
30 GET #2,J%
50 PRINT CVI(I1$), CVI(Q1$), CVS(E1$), G1$
55 J%=J%-1
60 IF J%>0 GOTO 30
70 CLOSE #1
80 END
```

Since there are 3 records in the file, we set J% to 3. The GET statement then retrieves the third record in the file, and line 50 prints that record. Line 55 decrements by one, and the GET statement retrieves the second record in the file. When J%=0, the loop terminates, the file is closed, and the program ends.

PROBLEM 9-23 Write a program that adds 1 to the quiz score of student #3 in the direct-access file STUDENT2.DAT.

Answer:

```
10 OPEN "R", 1, "STUDENT2.DAT"
20 FIELD #1, 2 AS I1$, 2 AS Q1$, 4 AS E1$, 1 AS G1$
30 GET #1, 3
40 LSET Q1$=MKI$(CVI(Q1$)+1)
50 PUT #1, 3
60 CLOSE #1
70 END
```

Line 30 retrieves the third record from the file, and line 40 adds 1 to that record. In line 40, the function CVI converts the string value stored in Q1$ to an integer value so that 1 can be added to it. Then MKI$ converts the incremented integer value to string form so that it can be returned to the direct-access file.

PROBLEM 9-24 Modify the program in Problem 9-23 so that it prompts the user to enter the record to be updated.

Answer:

```
10 OPEN "R", 1, "STUDENT2.DAT"
20 FIELD #1, 2 AS I1$, 2 AS Q1$, 4 AS E1$, 1 AS G1$
25 INPUT "ENTER THE RECORD TO CHANGE", R%
30 GET #1, R%
40 LSET Q1$=MKI$(CVI(Q1$)+1)
50 PUT #1, R%
60 CLOSE #1
70 END
```

We can use a variable as the record number in the PUT and GET statements.

PROBLEM 9-25 What is the output of the following program

```
10 OPEN "I", 1, "TEST.DAT"
20 INPUT #1, NAME$, STATE$
30 PRINT NAME$, STATE$
40 CLOSE #1
50 END
```

if the file TEST.DAT contains the following data?

```
"BUNYAN, PAUL", "MINNESOTA"
```

Answer:

```
BUNYAN, PAUL    MINNESOTA
```

Because the string data are properly enclosed in quotes, the data are preserved as intended.

PROBLEM 9-26 What is the output of the program in Problem 9-25 if the file TEST.DAT has the following data?

```
BUNYAN, PAUL, "MINNESOTA"
```

Answer:

```
BUNYAN     PAUL
```

Since the string BUNYAN, PAUL is not enclosed in quotes, the comma becomes a delimiter rather than a piece of data.

PROBLEM 9-27 What is the output of the following program?

```
10 OPEN "R", 4, "JUNK.DAT"
20 FIELD #4, 10 AS A$, 10 AS B$
30 RSET A$="FIRST"
40 LSET B$="SECOND"
50 PRINT A$;B$
60 CLOSE
70 END
```

Answer:

```
FIRSTSECOND
```

Since RSET places the string at the right of a field and LSET at the left, the strings will be printed next to each other.

PROBLEM 9-28 What is the output of the program in Problem 9-27 if we change lines 30 and 40 to

```
30 LSET A$="FIRST"
40 RSET B$="SECOND"
```

Answer:

```
FIRST       SECOND
```

Line 30 places the string "FIRST" at the left of field A$, and line 40 places "SECOND" at the right of field B$. The result is that the values are printed as shown.

PROBLEM 9-29 What is the output of the following program?

```
10 OPEN "R", 6, "JUNK.DAT"
20 FIELD #6, 12 AS Z$
30 LSET Z$="THIS IS A TEST"
40 PRINT Z$
50 CLOSE
60 END
```

Answer:

```
THIS IS A TE
```

Line 20 creates a field that is 12 bytes long. However, line 30 assigns a 14-character string to that field. The result is that the last two characters of the string are truncated.

PROBLEM 9-30 What is the output of the program in Problem 9-29 if you change line 30 to

```
30 RSET Z$="THIS IS A TEST"
```

Answer:

```
IS IS A TEST
```

RSET places the string in the rightmost portion of Z$. Since the string is two characters too long for the field, the two leftmost characters are truncated.

PROBLEM 9-31 What is the output of the following program?

```
10 OPEN "R", 6, "JUNK.DAT"
20 FIELD #6, 12 AS Z$
30 LSET Z$="THIS IS"
35 RSET Z$="A TEST"
40 PRINT Z$
50 CLOSE
60 END
```

Answer:

    A TEST

LSET and RSET completely overwrite the entire contents of a field, filling in any unused positions with blanks. In this program, both LSET and RSET are used with Z$. In line 30, LSET places "THIS IS" in the leftmost position of Z$. However, in line 35, RSET places "A TEST" in the rightmost position of Z$, which overwrites the data assigned by LSET.

PROBLEM 9-32 What is wrong with the following program?

```
1Ø INPUT #1, X,Y
2Ø OPEN "I", 1, "NOFILE"
3Ø PRINT X,Y
4Ø END
```

Answer: A file must first be opened before data can be read from or written to it.

10 *GRAPHICS AND SCREEN CONTROL*

THIS CHAPTER IS ABOUT

☑ **Programming Screen Displays**
☑ **Text Displays**
☑ **Graphics Characters**
☑ **Low Resolution Graphics**
☑ **High Resolution Graphics**
☑ **Sprite and Shape Graphics for Animation**

10-1. Programming Screen Displays

Personal computers typically use a television set or specially designed video monitor as their main output device. Televisions and monitors are extremely useful and versatile, supporting both textual and graphic output in a variety of creative and interesting ways. Unfortunately, there is considerable variation among different versions of BASIC as to the statements that are used for screen control and graphics. However, although the form of these statements will differ, the functions they perform are reasonably consistent. In general, there are five modes in which screen displays can be used:

1. Text display
2. Graphics characters
3. Low resolution graphics
4. High resolution graphics
5. Shape and sprite graphics for animation

10-2. Text Display

Text displays vary among different computers in terms of the number of characters displayed per line, the number of lines displayed on the screen, and the capacity to display lower-case letters. In general, the more expensive computers can display more text per screen. Typical screen display sizes are 24 or 25 lines of 40 characters each, 16 lines of 64 characters each, and 25 lines of 80 characters each.

A. Character display

1. Characters are usually placed on the screen by PRINT statements, but may be placed directly into memory by POKE statements or machine-language routines. A special area of memory is reserved for the screen display; characters stored in these locations are displayed in the corresponding screen locations.
2. Some computers permit the programmer to specify specialized text attributes such as the color of the text, inverse text (black letters on a white background), flashing text, and underlined text. These attributes may be implemented by special characters embedded in the text which do not themselves print but which control the printing of the characters that follow. Some versions of BASIC provide statements to produce these effects.

B. Cursor control

1. Each version of BASIC has a statement that clears the display screen and positions the cursor in the upper left-hand corner. Two common examples of this statement are HOME and CLS (for CLear Screen).

2. It is often desirable to position the cursor at a specific location on the screen so that text to be printed may be placed exactly where desired. One technique is to provide special statements to position the cursor. For example, Apple II Applesoft® BASIC provides the statements HTAB (to position the cursor at a particular column) and VTAB (to position the cursor at a particular line). For example, to print "HELLO" on line 5, starting in position 10, you could write Applesoft® statements as follows:

```
100 VTAB 5
110 HTAB 10
120 PRINT "HELLO"
```

3. Another statement that is used on some systems to position the cursor is PRINT @. In effect, this is a PRINT statement that also specifies the position of the cursor. For example, the statement

```
230 PRINT @400, "HELLO"
```

will display characters beginning with the 400th character. The syntax of the PRINT @ statement varies among versions of BASIC.

10-3. Graphics Characters

Some personal computers have special graphics characters that can be intermixed with normal text characters and used to create charts, tables and simple graphics. The advantage of such characters is the ease with which they can be used; often, they can be incorporated into standard PRINT statements. Thus, text and graphics can be freely intermixed, which is not always possible in low and high resolution graphics. The disadvantage in using these characters is that they are usually limited to a particular model of computer, which makes it difficult to transfer programs that contain these characters to a different computer.

10-4. Low Resolution Graphics

Most personal computers offer low resolution graphics. This type of graphics display consists of small squares that are arranged on the screen to create various patterns and designs. Because low resolution graphics are created with small squares, they cannot produce smooth curves.

In Applesoft® BASIC, the command GR sets the computer to low resolution mode, which in effect divides the display screen into an array consisting of 40 by 48 boxes. The statement COLOR $= n$ is used to select 1 of 16 possible colors (n must be a value between 0 and 15). The command PLOT x,y draws a square, in the last specified color, at position x,y in the array on the display screen. Applesoft® graphics also provides the statements HLIN and VLIN to draw horizontal and vertical lines in low resolution graphics.

10-5. High Resolution Graphics

High resolution graphics provide the most detailed graphics available on personal computers. Although the quality of these graphics is still far less than the quality available on more expensive systems, when used proficiently these graphics can produce creative and interesting results.

1. On the Apple II® computer, the command HGR is used to set the computer to high resolution graphics mode. In this mode the computer divides the display into an array consisting of 280 by 160 dots. The command HPLOT x,y places a dot at position x,y. With the inclusion of additional operands, this statement may be extended to print lines and complex line figures. Such a statement might appear as follows:

> HPLOT *x1,y1* TO *x2,y2* TO *x3,y3* . . .

2. The IBM® Personal Computer provides the statement SCREEN n, where n is used to select a medium resolution mode (320 by 200 dots) or a high resolution mode (640 by 200 dots). IBM® BASIC provides a number of special graphics statements, including the following:

> CIRCLE
> COLOR
> DRAW
> PAINT
> LINE

10-6. Sprite and Shape Graphics for Animation

Some personal computers, including the Apple II®, Commodore 64®, and IBM®PC, provide special graphics called *sprite*, or *shape*, graphics that can be used to produce animation. With sprite graphics, the shape or design of an object is stored in an array according to the rules of the particular computer system being used. A special statement specifying both the array and the screen position automatically draws the object on the screen. When the statement is executed a second time, the object is erased. Then, by changing the screen location, the object can be redrawn in a different position on the screen. On the Apple II®, the statement

> XDRAW s AT x,y

draws pre-stored shape s at screen position x,y. The IBM® PC uses the statement

> PUT (x,y), *array*

to draw *array* at position x,y.

RAISE YOUR GRADES

Can you explain . . . ?

☑ the difference between low resolution and high resolution graphics
☑ how graphics characters can be used to produce charts and tables
☑ how to clear the display screen
☑ how to position the cursor at a desired location
☑ how sprite (or shape) graphics are used to produce animation

SUMMARY

1. The most commonly used output device for personal computers is the standard television or video monitor. Televisions and monitors permit various displays to be programmed, including text, graphics, and animation.
2. There are five display modes commonly found in personal computers: (1) text (2) graphics characters (3) low resolution graphics (4) high resolution graphics (5) sprite or shape graphics.
3. Text displays vary among computers in terms of the number of lines of text available, the number of characters per line, the availability of lower-case letters, and special character attributes such as inverse (reverse) display and underlining. Some computers offer special graphics characters that can be used to produce graphs, charts, and simple graphic displays.
4. Each version of BASIC has a statement used to clear the screen of text and position the cursor at the upper left-hand corner. Typical statements are CLS and HOME.
5. Many versions of BASIC have statements that position the cursor at a desired print position on the screen. Typical statements are VTAB and HTAB (Apple®) and PRINT @ (TRS-80®).

6. Low resolution graphics divides the screen into an array of squares that are used to create various patterns and designs.
7. High resolution graphics divides the screen into an array of small dots, which provides finer detail than is possible in low resolution graphics.
8. Sprite or shape graphics permit pre-defined objects to be drawn, erased, and redrawn on the screen; this permits animated displays.

RAPID REVIEW   Answers

True or False?

1.	Low resolution graphics permits smooth curves to be drawn.	False
2.	Sprite graphics is used for animated displays.	True
3.	Special graphics characters may be mixed with ordinary text on many personal computers.	True
4.	CLS and HOME are typical cursor commands.	True
5.	High resolution graphics divides the screen into an array of small squares.	False

Fill in the blanks

1.	Characters are usually displayed on the screen by _____ statements.	PRINT
2.	The command CLS (or HOME) will _____ the display screen.	clear
3.	_____ can be incorporated into standard PRINT statements to produce simple graphics.	Graphics characters
4.	With _____ graphics, the screen is divided into small dots.	high resolution
5.	With _____ graphics, the screen is divided into small squares.	low resolution

INDEX

Page numbers in italics refer to solved problems.